# tots
## ARE NON DIVORCEABLE
### A WORKBOOK FOR DIVORCED PARENTS AND THEIR CHILDREN

**AGES BIRTH TO 5 YEARS**

SARA BONKOWSKI, PH.D.

ACTA
ASSISTING CHRISTIANS TO ACT
PUBLICATIONS

To my son and daughter, Brian and Karla,
and my stepdaughters, Kim and Kelly

*TOTS ARE NONDIVORCEABLE*
*A Workbook for Divorced Parents and Their Children*
*Ages Birth to 5 Years*
BY SARA BONKOWSKI, Ph.D.

Dr. Bonkowski is Professor of Social Work at Aurora University in Aurora, Illinois, and the founder of the Myrtle Burks Center for clinical social work in Glen Ellyn, Illinois. She is the author of *Kids Are Nondivorceable* and *Teens Are Nondivorceable*.

Edited by Patrice J. Tuohy
Cover Design by Isz
Typesetting by Garrison Publications

Copyright ©1998 by Sara Bonkowski
Published by   ACTA Publications
                4848 N. Clark Street
                Chicago, IL 60640
                800-397-2282

Library of Congress Catalog number: 97-77685
ISBN: 0-87946-178-0
Printed in the United States of America
02 01 00 99 98 5 4 3 2 1 First Printing

# CONTENTS

## Acknowledgements

Writing *Tots Are Nondivorceable* has been a solitary experience. I spent many hours alone with child development texts, reflecting on the experiences of countless divorcing parents who have shared their lives with me. Creating plans for their situations and learning what worked for their little ones helped me develop the ideas, examples, recommendations, and exercises presented in this book. To all those parents, thank you for caring about your young children. Of course, all of the names and situations used in this book are fictional and any similarity to those of real people is purely coincidental.

Thanks to Aurora University and to my dean, Dr. Sandra Alcorn, who arranged for me to have a much needed year-long sabbatical to write this book. My appreciation also to Gregory Pierce and the staff of ACTA Publications for making available another book that promotes healing and health, this one for the divorced parents of very young children. Finally, my love to my husband, John Mulherin, who is a spectacular partner in all of my adventures.

# C H A P T E R 1

## BEGINNING TO REBUILD

"I don't think her father even knows how to change
a diaper or take her temperature, yet the judge said
Amy has to go with him every weekend."

—Fran, mother of 6-month-old Amy

Divorce is difficult for parents and their teen or school-age children, but divorcing parents with very young children have unique considerations. Amy's parents separated during the pregnancy; she never experienced her parents living together. Fran did not share Amy's birth with Bob; she came home to her apartment alone, alone to take care of a new baby. She often feels overwhelmed and tired, yet she is committed to her beautiful baby daughter. She is concerned about Amy's being away from her every other weekend, even if it is only Saturday afternoon through Sunday morning. Fran worries whether Bob will hear Amy cry at night. Can he comfort her? Is Amy missing her mother?

Bob is worried, too. He doesn't even know his baby daughter. If he doesn't begin to see her soon, he is afraid Amy will never know her father. Bob has never taken care of an infant, and he is hoping he will be able to do everything right. Just to be sure, he is planning on taking Amy to his parents' house until he feels more comfortable with her care.

Amy can't talk. She doesn't know what is going on. She doesn't understand divorce. So, unlike her parents, Amy can't tell anyone how she is feeling. Grown-ups (parents, judges, and attorneys) making divorce-related decisions about infants and toddlers can plan better if they understand the needs of Amy and other young children.

All parents of young children report that the demands are exhausting. When the human infant is born, every survival need must be provided for by someone else, but by the time he or she turns 5, the child is ready for kindergarten, knows colors, is learning to tie shoes, ride a bike with training wheels, play with friends, and can recite the time of a favorite TV show. The years between birth and 5 are physically and emotionally demanding for the parents—years of helping the child master all of the emerging new tasks, years of interrupted sleep, years of postponing personal adult needs.

But to parents, the joy of seeing their child smile, hearing new sounds that turn into words, watching as toddling becomes walking, observing the innocence of peaceful sleep are rewards that can't be described. All of the work and inconvenience is worth it. Parents who divorce during their child's first five years have all of the challenging demands and joys of raising a young child while, at the same time, they experience the end of their marriage and try to make important decisions about the future. If you are in this situation this book is for you. It is written for both mothers and fathers, because your child needs both parents.


## DIFFERENT FAMILIES

Divorcing families with young children are not all alike. Some parents divorce when they only have *one child*. Like Amy's parents, they may divorce during the pregnancy or the first year after birth. These parents have no history or experience in parenting and have not parented together. Parents who never married may be facing some of the same concerns as parents who divorce with a young infant.

Other divorces take place when parents have *two or three children under 5*. These parents experience an overload of demands. Each of the children needs slightly different care. If there has been stress, anger, and sadness in the months preceding the separation, both parents may be emotionally depleted from the breakup and caring for infants, toddlers, or preschoolers.

Some divorcing parents have a *young child and older children*. These parents usually have a longer history of parenting together and the older children may provide some help and support for the infant. However, the older children have their own needs and interests that must be taken into consideration.

Or a divorce takes place when the parents' marriage is a second marriage. They have a *young child, but there are older children from the first marriage* of one or both parents.

Throughout this book ideas and suggestions will be made that are based on what is best for very young children. Please keep in mind that each divorcing family is complex. Think about your family and your children. Use any ideas that will help in your situation.

Just as there are different families, the ages from birth to 5 represent fluid developmental stages. Entire books have been written about just the first six months of life. Therefore, it is difficult to summarize the major factors divorcing parents must consider when planning for their child. This is not a book on child development; there are plenty of excellent ones at the library or bookstore. However, basing decisions on your child's emotional and intellectual capacity is critical.

To help you focus on your child's needs at each age range, the discussions and exercises at the end of each chapter are organized into three developmental blocks of time: Infants (birth to 14 months), Toddlers (15 months to 2½ years), and Preschoolers (2½ to 5 years).

## INFANTS (BIRTH TO 14 MONTHS)

A sleeping infant, fresh from a bath, is relaxed and contented after a feeding. As he or she crawls around the floor, the infant's world begins to expand. Pulling up to the table, the baby sees wonderful treasures, but suddenly he or she falls, struggles up, and tries again. These are snapshots of this developmental stage. There are other pictures: fretful crying during the night, high temperatures, fearful clinging when a stranger speaks—all scenes of an infant making a beginning into life. Many important things happen during the first year that lay down patterns in the developing brain that will influence the child for the rest of her or his life. Probably the most important process that is being formed is the capacity for relationships. Is the world a safe place? Can I trust others?

To the very young child the world is experienced through the senses: sight, smell, taste, touch, sound. The child is not born knowing concepts like *mother, father,* or *cozy crib.* These concepts are sensed: mother smells a certain way, her voice sounds soft or harsh. The baby's response to the soft voice is: "All is okay. I'm safe," to the angry voice, "I am not safe." Dad is different from mother—his clothes smell different, his hands are bigger, his voice is deeper. Different nerve endings of excitement are stimulated. The baby's crib, the baby's room, the family routine are all experienced and sensed by the young child. The child's well-being is dependent on these important people and props being there for him or her. The sounds of fighting parents is frightening.

## TODDLERS (15 MONTHS TO 2½ YEARS)

Between 12 to 17 months, most children begin to walk. At the same time they are beginning to put words to things they see in their world: *doggie* (all dogs and cats), *wawa* (water), *nah* (bed), and so on. Parents continue to help the child master and feel safe in the world. They encourage the emerging skills, "Look at Billy walk; he's a big boy." "Here's the water. Water." Parents speak their toddler's language. If parents divorce when the child is a toddler, the child will feel the change. The routine is different; something is wrong. Where is Mom? Where is Dad? It is important for the toddler to experience her or his world as secure and dependable.

## PRESCHOOLERS (2½ TO 5 YEARS)

Between 2 and 3, the child has a growing sense that he or she is a separate person and possesses power to do things, to make things happen. The preschooler can open a drawer and pull out cookies, turn on the TV, climb out of the crib. The young preschooler can say no and get everyone upset. What a world! The infant needed survival care; now the preschooler is learning that he or she is not dependent on caretakers for everything. The child is testing to see whether he or she can be independent: Am I a person who can do things?

Preschoolers, of course, cannot take care of themselves, but they must try. Parents need to encourage these new skills but be there to protect their preschoolers and comfort them in their failures. Children of this age know much more than younger children, but they often use words that they don't really understand—they fool grown-ups. For example, 4-year-olds may use the word *divorce*. "We're divorced," they'll say. When asked, "Do you know what divorce means?" They'll nod yes: "It is parents fighting" or "It is when we moved to grandma's."

This is perfect understanding for a preschooler, but parents cannot depend on their 4- or 5-year-old to be totally reliable sources of information. They report the immediate; they use words that may not mean what adults mean when they use the same words. This is not to say that parents shouldn't listen to their preschoolers, they should. But parents must understand the whole picture. When a 4-year-old reports that "Mommy is mean to me," she may be telling her father that Mommy made her go to bed last night when she wanted to stay up and play. This is very important to remember when planning the child's time with each parent.

# TELLING YOUR CHILD ABOUT DIVORCE

If your child is very young, under 10 months old, there is nothing you can tell him or her about divorce. Of course, you will explain about the divorce to your child as he or she is able to understand. For the infant the most important thing you can do is create a stable, predictable home. Not always an easy task, especially when you are going through a divorce. Your toddler will miss Daddy or Mommy. About the time the one parent usually comes home, you may notice your toddler begins to search for the absent parent. At any noise he or she may say, "Da, Da?" You need to tell your toddler, "Daddy lives at grandma's now. You will see Daddy tomorrow" (or whenever the child will see Daddy or Mommy). With young children, as with the older children, always tell the truth as they are able to understand it.

The preschooler can understand a little more about divorce. When you separate, you can tell your preschooler, "Mommy and Daddy are getting a divorce. Daddy won't live with us. He is living in an apartment, and you will go visit him." With a child this age it helps to act out the divorce with little toy figures. First, have a wedding, with the parents and a minister (priest or judge). Tell the child that to form their family Mom and Dad got married. Then add the child and other children to the family, explaining that Mom and Dad had these children. Next, as the story goes, Mom and Dad decided they could not be married any more so they got a divorce. Mom and Dad go to a judge, and the judge tells them they aren't married any more, *but* they are still parents. The children figures are a family with Dad, and they are a family with Mom. Children like this experience because it provides a visual picture for what they have been told in words.

# THE PROCESS OF ADJUSTING

Rebuilding a family after a divorce is difficult and painful. Each family member will experience many changes and losses. Your young child will not grow up in the type of family you had hoped for, and you may feel some stigma about being a divorced parent. Although divorce is no longer an unusual phenomenon, it can still carry a negative connotation for those involved, especially parents with very young children.

What are some of the common ideas that divorcing parents of young children believe others think about them? Some divorcing parents will have others say to them, "You didn't try hard enough. You got married too quickly. You're not responsible." Many of these statements come from their parents, in-laws, or friends. It is difficult to begin to heal from a divorce when loved ones are critical.

Perhaps you did marry too quickly. Perhaps you married because of an unplanned pregnancy, and you hoped the marriage would be successful. These are unfortunate experiences; however, you have a very good reason to make thoughtful, responsible decisions now. You have a child who is going to need your love, interest, and support for a long time. It is good for everyone when a troubled marriage can be helped, but every marriage cannot be saved. Learn from the past; don't become paralyzed by what others think. If you decide that divorce is the most responsible action, continue acting responsibly throughout the divorce by considering your child's well-being in every decision.

Another disconcerting part of adjustment are the legal proceedings and the terms used in divorce—*plaintiff, defendant, fees, alimony, custody, noncustodial parent, parenting plan.* How awful it feels to have these terms applied to oneself. Your family is not just a legal entity, but a very personal, unique structure. Although the terms may make you feel like a cog in court proceedings, the concepts have been designed by the judicial system and state legislatures to protect you and your children. While it is important to look at legal realities in a human and caring manner, the fact is that there are legal constraints and limits for each parent and each child.

The ideas and suggestions in the following chapters have been gathered from several sources. As a clinical social worker, I see families—children and parents—in family and individual therapy. I have facilitated adjustment groups for divorcing adults and lead Saturday-morning groups for children whose parents are separated or divorced. I work with some families from the time they first begin to contemplate divorce and with other families who come for help only after years of bitter postdivorce hostilities. I am a Registered Custody Evaluator and a practitioner member of the Academy of Family Mediators.

Many of the case illustrations are drawn from these clinical experiences. To preserve anonymity, I have, of course, used fictitious names and have altered other identifying information relating to the children and families. Some of my past and present clients may think that they recognize their children or family situations, but that is only because many actual divorce situations, conflicts, and struggles are remarkably similar. In addition to my firsthand experience in helping divorcing families, I study, teach college classes, and conduct research on family and divorce. Finally, I am a parent with two children, and I personally experienced divorce almost 22 years ago. Some of my close friends have divorced, and we have shared with each other—as good friends do—our own reactions to divorce. I have observed the adjustment of my own children and my friends' children to divorce. This book is, therefore, an integration of clinical, scholarly, and personal experience.

Divorce is often such a difficult trauma for all family members that it may feel like things will never be normal again. It is important for your young developing child that you regain a positive outlook. Draw on any resource that is helpful—this book should be but one of your resources. Others may include your family, friends, religious faith, and community.

## THE EXERCISES

At the end of each chapter you will find exercises for you and for your child. The exercises for you will help you clarify the issue for yourself before you begin working with your child. Where needed, an example of how to do your exercise is provided. The exercises for children will be divided into ideas for Infants, Toddlers, and Preschoolers. Because children under 2 cannot participate in activities that promote a cognitive understanding of divorce, many of the exercises will simply be fun activities for you to do with your infant. The topics in the book are arranged in an order that will be most helpful in the rebuilding process:

- understanding how divorce losses affect parents, which in turn may affect the young child;

- discussing each age group (infant, toddler, preschooler) with suggestions for parenting plans for each age group;

- exploring special concerns, such as lifestyle issues and geographic separations;

- avoiding pitfalls, such as stopping child support or losing contact with your children;

- looking at the extended family as a resource;

- dealing with the difficult issues of parental dating and remarriage;

- planning for the future of your child and understanding how parental divorce continues to be an important influence throughout your child's life.

## WHICH PARENT?

This book is written especially for mothers and fathers. Grandparents and other interested parties, such as stepparents, may also find it useful in understanding parental divorce and how it affects the infant, toddler, and preschooler. Three major themes run throughout the book:

- A child needs a relationship with both parents.

- Parenting plans for young children should take into account each child's age; plans must change as the child's abilities change.

- Parents, not the legal system, are in the best position to make plans for their children.

If both parents express an interest in reading this book, it could stimulate ideas and open up the possibility of creating flexible but realistic parenting plans. However, if you and your former (or soon to be former) spouse have a mistrustful, hostile relationship, he or she may resent you telling him or her what to read. In that case, use the ideas yourself; you may be surprised at how much power you have to help improve the way you resolve differences. Unfortunately, there are some parents who, for various reasons, may be unable to actively participate in parenting their young children. Examples include a parent who is addicted to alcohol or drugs; an unpredictable, psychotic parent; an uncontrollably violent parent; a parent who plans to abduct the child; or a parent who shows no interest in his or her child. These instances are rare, but if this describes your situation, please get help for you and your child from a qualified mental-health professional—a social worker, psychologist, or psychiatrist.

## BEGINNING TO REBUILD

Use this book to understand yourself, your divorce experience, and your young child. Understand how these three elements are tied together. Remember, the adjustment process will take a considerable period of time. The essential fact to keep in mind is that the path of adjustment is never steady and you may have to work on it over and over. On the other hand, by the time you finish this book, you may be surprised at how much progress you and your child (or children) have made. Some of the exercises for parents may be revealing. Be as honest as you can when doing them; no one will be reading your answers. Only by being honest with yourself can you begin to truly recover from the divorce.

# EXERCISE 1

*Defining your strengths*

## FOR PARENTS

All divorces require that parents draw upon their strengths to help them reorganize and rebuild. Rebuilding after divorce in a family with very young children requires more energy, determination, and commitment than in families with older children. This is because young children require so much attention, and they are totally dependent on you. Your well-being and recovery is their well-being.

To begin the rebuilding process, it is important for you to identify your strengths and your child's strengths—those strengths will move you into the future.

Take out a piece of paper and along the left side list some of your strengths; don't be modest, you know yourself. List at least three. Beside each strength write how you think this strength will help you in rebuilding after the divorce. Now on another piece of paper write down three strengths of each of your children. How will these strengths help your child now and in the future?

After you complete the exercise, ask yourself what you discovered about yourself and your children.

### DOROTHY'S EXAMPLE

*Dorothy is the 25-year-old custodial mother of Taynia, 4½, and Joseph, 10 months, and has recently divorced from Tom.*

| MY STRENGTHS | HOW THEY WILL HELP |
|---|---|
| 1. Am a skilled bookkeeper | Can get a good job. |
| | Will keep track of own finances. |
| 2. Good cook | Will make good meals for Taynia and Joseph. |
| 3. Healthy | Hopefully I won't miss much work. |
| 4. Like the outdoors | Will do things outside when I begin to feel stress. |
| | Can find fun, inexpensive things to do with the children. |

| **TAYNIA'S STRENGTHS** | **HOW THEY WILL HELP** |
|---|---|
| 1. Makes friends easily | She will be able to have fun with her friends in school and in the neighborhood. |
| 2. Is cute | Her cute smile engages others; this should always help her with people. |
| 3. Likes her dance class | May turn into a true interest, but for now it helps her develop coordination and have fun. |

| **JOSEPH'S STRENGTHS** | **HOW THEY WILL HELP** |
|---|---|
| 1. Good eater and sleeper | Not being picky about food and able to sleep well will help him in adjustment (and help me, too). |
| 2. Beautiful brown eyes | Who can resist them? |
| 3. Very healthy | When he has to go to day care (if he does) maybe he can fight off germs. |

## DISCUSSION

First, Dorothy was surprised to realize that she could use her interests in cooking and the outdoors to help herself and her children in the rebuilding process. After doing the exercise she found herself reading some of her cookbooks and planning a picnic—something she hadn't done in a long time. Second, Dorothy was able to acknowledge that her skills in bookkeeping will be a real asset both in getting a job and taking charge or her own finances. Third, although being a healthy person never seemed that unusual, Dorothy realized that in having the responsibility for young children she is going to need to be healthy. She also noticed that she and Joseph are both healthy—a similarity.

Dorothy had always been proud of Taynia and her friendly, outgoing manner. Her former husband, Tom, has a similar personality, whereas Dorothy is more reserved. Doing this exercise allowed her to acknowledge Taynia's personality, even if it is like her father's. It gave Dorothy joy to write about how cute Taynia and Joseph are. Dorothy has been worried about having to go back to work full time; she would prefer to stay home until Joseph is at least 2. Just noticing how well-adjusted Joseph is allowed her to think that if she did have to go back to work, Joseph will probably be all right.

## EXERCISE FOR INFANTS

Take out a blanket or quilt and spread it out in the center of the floor. Put some bright colored blocks or other safe toys on the blanket. Now sit down on the blanket with your child. Tell the baby this is the *magic play blanket*. The baby won't understand what this means, but he or she will like the sound of your voice, the feel of the blanket, and the look on your face. Watch how your child plays. Lie down so you can look at you infant's face. Let your child initiate the play, but respond.

After 15 to 20 minutes, fold up the magic blanket. Now you and your infant can resume other activities. This is fun to do every once in a while. Your child will begin to look forward to the magic blanket.

## EXERCISE FOR TODDLERS

Sit on the floor or couch with your toddler. Take a towel and cover up a little stuffed toy. Say, "Where is Tabby?" See whether your child picks up the towel. Then cover other things and ask where they are? Put the towel over your head. "Where is Mommy (Daddy)?" Then put the towel over your toddler's head, "Where is Leon?" Toddlers love this game. They are learning that just because something is covered, it is not gone forever.

## EXERCISE FOR PRESCHOOLERS

Walk to a neighborhood playground with your preschooler. Watch how your child plays. What do you notice about him or her? Do you think that any of the other children at the playground are from divorced families? Why or why not? Observe your own perceptions about other families.

# C H A P T E R 2

## DIVORCE MEANS MANY CHANGES AND LOSSES

"It makes me so sad to think that four years ago we
were planning our wedding."

—Frank, father of 2-year-old Jake

Twenty-five-year-old Frank was overwhelmed by sadness at the breakup of his
3½ year marriage to Kate. He admits that he made mistakes. After work he often
went out to play darts and drink beer with the work crew. He also enjoyed watching
football with the guys. At first Kate asked him to come home, then she cried, then
they fought, finally she was quiet. One night when he came home, Kate and Jake
weren't there. A note said she had gone to her parents and was filing for divorce. No
amount of talking, even begging, would bring Kate back. Frank sees Jake twice a
week at Kate's mother's house. Kate tries not to be there when he comes. Frank is
attending a divorce adjustment group—he wants to get over the hurt; he wants to
learn from this marriage.

About 45 percent of first marriages end in divorce, and 60 percent of second
marriages also wind up in divorce court. These alarming statistics point to the reality that many parents and children will experience divorce. Regardless of the high
number of people who go through divorce, each family and each breakup has its
own sadness. When most people marry, they do not say "I do" to a statement that
asks whether they will remain married until they decide to divorce. Rather, each

bride and groom pledges to be married to the other "until death us do part." The couple envisions that they will be together for life; this vision may include raising children, having grandchildren, and eventually supporting each other through old age. Thus, when a marriage becomes untenable the husband and wife lose a deeply treasured dream.

In addition, all divorcing people face the loss of a social and sexual partner. Finding the energy, time, and trust necessary to find a new partner is difficult, especially when most of your time is consumed with taking care of young children. Many divorced women with young children say that when an eligible man finds out they have young children, he loses interest in the relationship. Statistics back up these reports; divorced fathers remarry at a much higher rate than mothers with children.

Another unique stress that divorcing parents of very young children face is that divorce leaves the residential parent with the daily responsibility of taking care of a young child without having another adult available to provide relief and support. Moreover, most young families are just beginning to build careers, so dividing the limited resources between two homes often leaves both parents financially stretched.

If you are reading this book you probably see your own struggles in the above discussion. This chapter explores the reality of your losses and will help you continue to assess your strengths and resources to rebuild a happy future for you and your children.

## LOSS OF THE OTHER PARENT AS AN ACCESSIBLE HELPER

During pregnancy a woman turns inward; she is listening to her baby. This is natural and normal; parents feel a need to protect their offspring. The human infant requires much care to survive. Beginning to care for your child before he or she is born helps your child's survival rate. Some expectant fathers may feel abandoned or shut out. Divorcing parents often report that things changed when the baby was born. Currently fathers are routinely included in many prenatal parent-education classes and are encouraged to take part in the birth experience. This procedure is designed to help the new dad bond with the new baby and be part of the experience. Despite these programs, which have helped fathers, mothers, and babies bond, a baby lives inside the mother for nine months. The two are never apart. The baby grows hearing the mother's voice and knows the mother's biological rhythms. The attachment between mother and child begins before birth and is physiological as well as psychological.

When a baby comes home from the hospital, the mother and child need a safe, protected environment. Enter Dad. The role of the father, in addition to pinch-hitting for an exhausted mother, is to take care of business. This means that the father worries about the money to pay the rent; he answers the phone; he runs to the pharmacy. The father protects the mother and baby, so the mother is free to feed, bathe, and cuddle her newborn.

Some male readers might be saying, "Hey, I am more involved with my child than my wife! In fact I think my baby is more bonded with me." Or female readers may be thinking that to assume that the woman has to do all of the caretaking is just buying into social roles designed to keep women dependent on men. In fact, some fathers *are* more attached, more nurturing by nature, than some mothers. Men can, and should, do many caretaking activities. Recent child-development studies cite the important role the father has in the healthy development of the child. Fathers stimulate the brain of a child in a way that is different from a mother's stimulation. A child needs both parents.

But we are biological beings, and the fact that in the first few years most infants and young children are more emotionally attached to their mothers than to their fathers is natural. The fact that the mother and infant need the father to care for them is also normal. Understanding and accepting your biological nature will help you in planning for your child.

When parents divorce during the first year or two of the child's life, the natural order of development is disrupted. The infant usually resides with the mother (although not always). So the mother alone must do all of the nurturing, cuddling, and feeding *and* pay the bills, fix the dripping faucet, go to work, do the washing. She needs help. When the father is with the child, he is often making decisions about child care alone. Should the 2-year-old take a nap? When is it all right to let the baby not finish a bottle? Is the child sick or just crabby? Often the father is unaware of the child's daily routine and subtle developmental changes.

An important and basic loss that divorcing parents of young children face is the loss of a partner to help them with all of the tasks involved in raising a child. No matter what age, children always need the love, attention, and care of both parents. However, when a child is older he or she can do many things independently; the parent has time to regroup psychologically and physically. With young children, the parent is always on call. Making plans that take into account both your child's needs and yours is the major focus of this book. Just because you are divorcing does not mean you can't raise a healthy child. You can.

## LOSS OF SPOUSE AND LOVER

Divorcing parents were lovers and marriage partners before they became parents. Having an adult partner to share life with—someone to come home to—is reassuring and supportive. Knowing that someone loves you and desires you sexually is exciting and can contribute to self-esteem. When a man and woman who happen to be parents divorce, they not only redefine how they will raise their children; they are adjusting to the loss of a lover. No longer are they going to be intimates. The loss of intimacy, both sexually and personally, can feel overwhelming. Be patient and kind to yourself, and you will heal from this loss.

## CHANGE IN FINANCIAL REALITY

Many divorcing parents with young children have been married less than ten years. If they married in their early 20s, starting their family two or three years later, then they may have been working at their jobs or developing their careers for about the same length of time as their marriage. During that time, typically, they both worked; when the first or second child is born, the mother often switches to part-time employment.

During the first ten years this typical young family often focuses on saving enough money to buy a house, a place to raise a family. If the marriage deteriorates and the couple decides to divorce, the family often faces the reality that there is not enough money for the mother to stay in the house with the children. Even if the mother decides to resume full-time work, there may not be enough money, even with child support, to pay the mortgage, utilities, car payment, food, doctor's bills, and child care. Child care for two children under 5 could well amount to $600 to $1,000 a month. The house is sold and after legal expenses and debts are paid there may be little money left over for the father and mother to start over. Some mothers take their young children and move in with their parents for a few years; grandparents may provide necessary baby-sitting and allow the mother the opportunity to save some money. Other mothers move to an apartment that may lack the conveniences of their house. Either option will require mothers and children to make lifestyle adjustments.

Often the father has difficulty adjusting to the changes in his finances, too. A father with two children under 5 may have to pay 25 to 30 percent of his income for child support, and he may be required to pay additional maintenance for a few years to help the mother achieve a more financially secure base. (Each state has its own guidelines for child support; the figures cited are representative.) Thus, the father sees a greatly reduced paycheck and may blame the mother for his fate.

Perhaps you are in a fortunate situation where there will be enough money for both parents to live as they did before the divorce. If that is the case, you will not be forced to make critical, urgent decisions based solely on money. But all divorcing parents feel the loss of their combined earnings and partnership. How to do more with less and at the same time be happy and available to your child? Quite a challenge, but it can be done. Those parents who decide to let go of their disappointments and enjoy each day are the ones who are happy, even if the apartment is not great or they have to shop at a resale store for their children's clothes. Remember that young children are not teenagers; they do not know whether their outfits were purchased at an upscale department store or the neighborhood secondhand shop.

## THE LEGAL SYSTEM

Most of us have very little contact with the legal system; thus, being a player in that system can be a stressful and unpleasant experience. When a divorce begins, the parties enter a world that seems distant, overwhelming, and powerful. Attorneys, judges, court personnel are comfortable with this world. They understand the lingo; they respond to the rituals. Divorcing parents may wonder, "Does anyone hear me? Do they really care what happens to my child?" The answers to these questions are yes and no. Attorneys hear the sad, angry stories of divorcing clients every day. They must be able to represent their clients well, so it is better for them not to become emotionally involved in each case. Your attorney hears you and cares, but your attorney has a job to do and must stay focused on the best possible judgment.

Domestic-relations judges sit and listen to parents fight over every aspect of their children's lives. Can Dad cut this child's hair? Can Mom spend the whole Sunday of Mother's Day with the children? Mom wants the children to attend her church; Dad wants them to go to his. Dad sends the children home with dirty clothes. Mom doesn't help the children with their homework. Mom doesn't think the children are safe when Dad drinks. Mom leaves the children alone to go out with her boyfriend. And on and on and on. This is the life of a judge who hears divorce cases. The problem with the legal system is that it is not designed to know your family and your children; it is designed to enforce statutes governing the dissolution of marriage. You and your former spouse are the two people who know your children best. You have more interest in their future than the court. You also have the power and capability to keep your case from going to trial and spending thousands of dollars in legal fees (which could be spent on your children). Divorcing parents can design their own parenting plans, which can be redesigned as the children's or parents' needs change.

One way you can have more input into the final parenting plan for your children is to work with a divorce mediator. A divorce mediator is a mental-health professional or attorney who has had special training in how to help parents work together to plan for their children. The mediator may also help with planning the division of property. After parents have agreed to what they want for their future, they consult with attorneys, and the attorneys take the final agreement into court with reduced acrimony and cost. A mediator is neutral; he or she will not tell you what to do but will help two disagreeing parents work out a plan. It is your plan.

Mediators can also be consulted if issues arise after your divorce. Frequently, in two or three sessions with a mediator parents can come to an agreement about their children. Parents who felt they couldn't even talk to each other leave knowing they can rise above personal pasts. They are not friends; they are responsible parents.

An issue that parents often fight about is custody. The terms *custodial* and *noncustodial* parent have bad connotations. It sounds as if one parent owns the children and the other only has limited rights. Parents do not like to feel excluded from their children's lives. In response to parents' dislike of the traditional custody concepts and in hopes of reducing litigation over the children, the courts came up with the concept of *joint custody*. Joint custody does not mean that the children live half of the time with each parent but that each parent has the right to decision making about their children. When parents are awarded joint custody, they submit a parenting plan that describes where the children will live and how the children will spend time with each parent. This plan is incorporated into the final divorce decree. Some of those plans look very much like the old-fashioned divorce settlements of visits every other weekend and two weeks in the summer. Others have complex schedules in which children are transferred several times a week. In some states joint custody is the preferred determination, and parents must make a case about why there shouldn't be joint custody. As beneficial as joint custody is, there have been problems when it is awarded to parents who cannot work together. When children witness high conflict between parents, their adjustment may be threatened; in these cases a more traditional custody decision may actually work best.

This discussion of custody concepts is included to help you familiarize yourself with options. The most important thing to remember is that *your young child has a right and need to know both parents.* As parents, you must make plans for this child for many years. How can you make this happen peacefully? You cannot control the other parent, you can only be responsible for yourself.

# TAKING CARE OF YOURSELF

Thinking back over your marriage and acknowledging the changes and losses divorce brings is an important step in healing. However, you cannot stop the world to mourn. As you go about your daily living, you will find some activities are more enjoyable than others. During the healing process you may find yourself doing more of whatever gives you comfort. For example, during a divorce many adults talk to friends on the phone more frequently and for longer periods of time than they had previously. Other methods of coping include getting new clothes, eating different foods, starting a workout program, playing new music, and getting a different haircut. These are all positive activities that may help you feel better during a stressful time.

Yet, there are other coping techniques that are not healthy. The overindulgent response includes: overeating, excessive use of alcohol, too much sleep, overspending, compulsive gambling, compulsive dieting. If you find yourself engaging in behavior that is potentially harmful to your health or security, please get professional help. Just talking with an outside party may help you develop better ways to comfort yourself. In most communities there are groups for parents going through divorce. These groups usually meet for eight to ten weeks and are open to all. Sometimes they meet in churches, libraries, or park district facilities. Most are offered at a reasonable fee. If you cannot afford the fee, discuss it with the group leader, and she or he may be able to make an adjustment. If there is no child care provided, ask a friend to share baby-sitting duties—he or she watches your children one evening, you watch his or hers on another.

Organizations such as Parents Without Partners, Young Single Parents, and New Beginnings were developed to meet the social and informational needs of divorcing adults. These organizations provide interesting speakers and sponsor dances and parties. If you know of such an organization in your area but feel hesitant attending, go to a program first. Listening to a speaker is much less scary than going to a dance. Attending a Bible study or prayer group or speaking individually with a minister, priest, or rabbi may help you draw on your spiritual strength. Ask others to pray for you. Pray for yourself, your child, and your former spouse.

Another healthy activity is participating in a parent-child activity. One divorced father enrolled in parent-child swim classes with his 3-year-old daughter. Not only did it give them something to do, but by the age of 5 the little girl was a very good swimmer. Call your local YWCA or YMCA and find out what they offer. If the cost is an obstacle, ask the program director about available scholarships.

# EXERCISE 2

*Acknowledging your losses*

## FOR PARENTS

Take out a large sheet of paper. At the top, write the words *Losses/Changes* and then write *Options for Healing*. Now write the name of each person in your family (including your former spouse) down the left side of the paper. List what you believe are the major losses and changes for each family member, and next to the changes write any suggestion you might have to help the person adapt and heal from these losses and changes caused by the divorce.

## TONY'S EXAMPLE

*Tony is the father of 4-year-old Sammy, who lives with Sammy's mother, Vicky.*

**TONY**

*LOSSES/CHANGES*

1. Loss of seeing Sammy every day.

2. Loss of face with family and friends.

3. Having someone else tell me what I have to pay my wife.

*OPTIONS FOR HEALING*

1. Plan things to do when he's with me. Read a book about 4-year-olds.

2. Remember I'm a good person even if divorced. Talk with a priest.

3. Accept the fact she is entitled to the money (this will be hard).

**VICKY**

*LOSSES/CHANGES*

1. Lost friends we had together.

2. Will have to go back to work when Sammy is 5.

3. She doesn't seem to be losing as much as me!

*OPTIONS FOR HEALING*

1. She is a friendly person. I'm sure she'll do okay.

2. I know Vicky wanted to be a stay-at-home Mom. I'm not sure what she can do.

3. Don't envy her.

| SAMMY | *LOSSES/CHANGES* | *OPTIONS FOR HEALING* |
|---|---|---|
| | 1. Losing growing up living with a mom & dad. | 1. Will have to help him feel okay about his new life. |
| | 2. Losing sharing many holidays with me. | 2. Try to make the holidays he is with me fun. |
| | 3. Doesn't get to see me every day. | 3. Realize he is okay. Call him between visits. |

## DISCUSSION

This was a difficult exercise for Tony to do, and he worked very hard at being honest with himself. He realized that in many ways he, Vicky, and Sammy were very lucky. His company was successful enough that Vicky and Sammy could stay in the family home, and he was able to buy himself a new townhouse. He had resented the fact that Vicky was in the house they designed and built, but when he shoved his bitterness aside he saw that Sammy was going to be required to make fewer changes than many other divorcing families.

Tony also realized that although Sammy missed him, much of Sammy's life was the same. Tony was far lonelier than Sammy. He had been calling Sammy several times a day, and as he completed the exercise he acknowledged that he was depending on his 4-year-old son to make him happy. This didn't seem good for Sammy. Tony decided to call Sammy every other day. If Tony felt lonely in between, he would visit his parents or play golf.

A final theme emerged. Tony was resentful and angry that Vicky had not wanted to stay married. Even though they had run into problems, he did not believe in divorce. No one in his family had ever been divorced, and he felt a stigma that somehow he should have been able to prevent the divorce. Tony was used to being in charge—he was the boss at work; now Vicky, her lawyer, and the judge were telling him what he could and could not do. This infuriated him. Luckily, Tony realized that as long as he was bitter and angry, he would not be a good father and would not be happy. He committed to talk with a priest for several sessions to help him resolve his pain.

## EXERCISE FOR INFANTS

Show your baby his or her image in the bathroom or bedroom mirror. Ask, "Who it is?" Then say, "That's Margaret" (or whatever your child's name is). Repeat this several times a week. Babies love it.

## EXERCISE FOR TODDLERS

Find a nonbreakable mirror that your toddler can lug around. Be sure it is not made of glass! Look in the mirror and say, "I see Daddy (or Mommy). Who do you see?" This is a fun activity to do with your little one.

## EXERCISE FOR PRESCHOOLER

Find some old magazines, especially family or home magazines. Sit down with your preschooler and say, "Let's look for houses that look like where Daddy lives and where Mommy lives." When you see a picture of a house, you can ask if that looks like where Daddy lives or where Mommy lives. Then you can tear out pictures that your child thinks look like Daddy's or Mommy's house. This is a good way to tell your child that she or he has two houses, and it also demonstrates your acceptance of the new living arrangement.

# CHAPTER 3

# INFANTS—KNOWING AND PLANNING FOR YOUR BABY

"I'm glad we're getting divorced when he is just a
baby, he will never miss having us together."

—Janice, mother of 8-month-old Charlie

It is often assumed that if parents divorce when the child is very young the divorce will not affect them. Nothing could be further from the truth. It is true that an 8-month-old infant will not have a recoverable memory of living with both parents. But an infant is very vulnerable to the emotional process and the change in family routine associated with parental divorce. This chapter is designed to help you feel what an infant experiences during parental divorce. It will help you in making parenting plans if you are able to put yourself in your baby's shoes.

## THE BABY'S WORLD

When a baby is born a miracle happens—a new life comes into being, a life that has wonderful, amazing possibilities. However, a baby is not born with the initial capacity to understand the world or how to take care of himself or herself; your baby will need time and support to develop his or her capacity, skills, and knowledge. Abilities change and develop as the infant grows.

27

The first year of life is critical because the baby's brain is developing rapidly. Patterns and connections are being made that will influence behavior for the rest of the child's life. People can change, but feelings and behaviors that are established early in life are difficult to modify. The baby does not *understand* what is going on in his or her life, but he or she *senses* what is happening. Many developmental experts believe that the ability to form trusting relationships is established in the first two years of life.

To understand how this happens, let's look at some scenes from the life of a 4-month-old girl. The infant feels hungry, uncomfortable. She cries and fusses. Her mother comes and picks her up, already she feels happier, because she knows the sound of her mother's voice and her smell; she associates these with satisfaction. The mother changes the baby; the baby still fusses because she feels uncomfortable or hungry. She is given the breast or bottle at last—now she feels contentment and safety. Snuggling, the warm feeling, the stimulation of her mother stroking her hand— all of these are registered in the baby's brain. Of course, the baby does not know the words to describe what she is feeling; she simply experiences the feelings.

Later the baby is put back into her crib. The sheets smell familiar, the view of the bars on her crib is familiar, her mother's voice is soothing. Again the baby has a sense of security—the world is a good place. Much of her safety is associated with the feel, touch, voice, response, and smell of her mother. This 4-month-old is experiencing the world as a safe and dependable place. Another voice comes into the room, a louder voice. The hands that pick her up feel different; the smell is different; her dad is home. She knows these feelings, too; they are more exciting feelings. Dad lifts her high; she smiles and kicks her feet. She is happy and excited by the deep voice and the firm hands. Dad is safe, too.

But then the parents separate as a prelude to divorce. The baby hears words, tones, fighting. These are not the words she has felt before. They are too loud, too harsh. Something is wrong. Her mother picks her up to nurse, but mother feels different. She does not feel happy; she feels anxious and sad. The baby feels what her mother feels. Although she is relieved to be fed, something has changed. The baby feels the anxiety; she frets. A day passes. The firm hands and deep voice do not pick her up. Her routine has changed; something is different. Although she is still fed and bathed, much of the joy is missing from her life.

Three months go by. Suddenly the baby is picked up by the big hands and taken away in the car. Who is this? She does not remember the voice, the touch, the smell of Dad. The baby is now 7 months old, and Dad is a stranger. She doesn't know his face (separation anxiety often starts between 7 and 9 months). She feels afraid; she does not experience security. The big hands give her a bottle; she is happy to eat, but she feels uneasy. This is not what she is used to. Fretful, she is searching for a familiar voice or touch. The big hands put her in a bed; it does not feel familiar; it does not smell the same. She cries, something is wrong. "Where is my mother, my crib, my safe world?" After a while she tires and falls asleep. Dad thinks she is adjusting, but she is withdrawing, waiting, searching for her security.

This, then, is the infant's world and how a baby may experience divorce—based on the best knowledge we have of child development.

## THE PARENT'S WORLD

Life changes for parents when a child is born, whether it is their first or fifth. Mothers report that they are not prepared for how tired they feel. The tiredness lasts almost two years. Some of the tiredness is from physical changes, but much of it has to do with the constant monitoring a mother does, day and night, as she listens for the infant. This is normal; it assures the child's survival. Fathers report they feel a new type of responsibility; they will need to care for the child until he or she is grown. In addition to these changes, the routine of the home changes. More work is added: mountains of dirty clothes to wash, beds to change, food to buy, doctor's appointments to make, another person's needs to include. But for most parents the joy of anticipating a baby and then working together to parent their new child helps them overcome the tiredness, responsibility, and other changes that accompany the birth of a baby.

For some parents, the stress of pregnancy or the addition of the new responsibilities is enough to push an already vulnerable marriage into divorce. Values related to parenting may never have been discussed, and when faced with these decisions the couple realizes that they don't really agree on important issues. Some new parents panic with the added responsibility and decide that they still want a single life. Drug problems, poverty, infidelity, or domestic violence may also pose a threat to the new child and family. These are the types of concerns that parents may be facing while caring for an infant and negotiating a divorce.

If you find yourself divorcing and you have an infant, it is important for you to take care of yourself and take care of your baby. Your baby needs you to be healthy. You are your child's most important asset. You are going to need the help of others. Ideally, the other parent will be your biggest support. But you will probably also need the help of grandparents, aunts and uncles, good neighbors, close friends.

# PRINCIPLES UNDERLYING PARENTING PLANS FOR INFANTS

*Frequent-Contact Plan.* Very young children need to have a secure, dependable routine. Unless absolutely necessary, they should not be separated from their mother (or primary caretaker) or from their known, secure environment for extended periods of time. To maintain a bond with the father (or nonresident spouse), the infant should have frequent but short visits with him. If possible, the father should take part in some of the daily caretaking routine. (If the father has been the primary caretaker for the child and provides the child's primary feelings of safety and security, the parenting plan should reflect that the baby reside with the father, and the mother should be the frequent helper. But in most families the mother has provided the primary caretaking of the infant, and it is important to keep the infant's routine as stable as possible.)

*The specifics of the frequent-contact plan:*

**1. No overnights until the child is 2½ to 3 years old.** The child will feel too worried and anxious away from its mother. This has nothing to do with the ability of the father to parent.

**2. The father sees child three to four (or more) times a week, preferably for two to three hours at a time.** The baby may not feel comfortable with the father if she or he sees him only once a week.

**3. For a few transition months following separation, the father comes into the mother's house some of the time to do bathing, tucking in, and so on.** This is an ideal arrangement but should not be attempted if there is fear of hostility, prying, or other unsafe conditions. The "father in the home" practice should never be imposed by the court, because if the parent's cannot agree on a routine they both feel comfortable with it will not work.

Some mothers have had their own mothers or friends present when a child's father comes, and then they use the time to grocery shop or run other errands. If this practice is possible, the child associates the father with security in the familiar home environment.

**4. No out-of-state or any other type of extended vacations until the child is older, preferably 5 or 6.**

Making the frequent-contact plan work takes considerable commitment and dedication to the child's welfare. It also takes two parents who can put aside their own needs, past hurts, and disappointments. This type of visitation lasts only until the child is between 2 and 3, then it can be revised.

# REACTIONS

*Fathers.* Some fathers feel angry that it is recommended to wait until the child is older for overnights, vacations, and other extended visits. They feel it is a negative judgment about men—that they cannot do as good a job as mothers. Some dads do not want any restrictions. This recommended plan has nothing to do with parents winning or losing but with the infant being provided for in a way that allows him or her to stay securely attached to both parents. If you are mainly interested in "winning," then your decisions may damage your child.

*Mothers.* Mothers often object to having to arrange so many visits each week. "We are getting divorced. I don't want to have to see him so much." They also worry that the dad will not know what to do with the baby. There is no question that having a schedule where the father sees the infant three to four times a week can be difficult for the mother. You may be very sad and distressed that the marriage ended, you may be angry and hurt about past events, you may be mistrustful. All of these feelings accompany divorce.

If you decide to use the frequent-contact plan, try to think of ways that will cut down on your having to have direct contact with your former spouse. Perhaps one night a week your brother, mother, or friend would be willing to come over for an hour or two. You can leave before he comes and return after he leaves. Or you can drop the infant off at the paternal grandmother's home, and your former spouse can arrive a little later. Or your former spouse can pick the child up at day care, and then you can pick the child up at his home.

These are just suggestions, you may be able to think of other arrangements. The key to the plan is that once it is made it stays the same for several months or a year (unless there is an emergency). If there are specific things the dad needs to know, just write a note. Many moms like the plan because they get breaks from all of the caretaking responsibilities, and they like the fact that they are promoting good father-child relationships.

# MORE THOUGHTS ABOUT VISITING PLANS

Every family is different. For example, if a baby has older siblings, he or she may be able to be away from the mother sooner and for longer periods. The presence of brothers and sisters represents the security of the baby's world. The key to a good plan is to take into account all aspects of your family. There are parents who are able to communicate well and make frequent-contact plans work. These parents can talk on the phone, respect each other as parents, and do not fear each other. Yet even willing and cooperative parents may need the help of a divorce mediator to provide a structure for them to discuss problems that may come up.

Unfortunately, there are situations where due to uncontrolled drug use, a history of violence, consuming jealousy, or continuing rage the frequent-contact plan is not recommended. If this describes your family, you will need legal and mental-health experts to help establish a safe plan. In all likelihood it will not include frequent visits and in some instances the visits may need to be supervised.

## TIPS ON INFANTS

Here are some things parents can do to ease the transition when the baby begins to be away from his or her primary home:

**1. Use the same blanket or toy at both homes.** This seems obvious, but some visiting parents think the blanket, binky, or stuffed doggie is too babyish. They say to themselves, "Now is my chance to make him a big boy (or girl)." Wrong! If you take away safe security items, you are causing your child considerable stress. Your child will associate bad feelings with you. There are many ways to help your baby, then toddler, then preschooler grow into a happy young boy or girl. Fighting his or her other parent over attachment toys is not one.

**2. Give the baby any prescribed medicines, and follow any other health regime that the residential parent suggests.** If you have a concern about the health care of your baby, make an appointment and discuss it with the physician. Be willing to pay for this consultation; become a cooperative, knowledgeable parent. Do not disregard the other parent's list of health procedures.

**3. Try to follow the infant's schedule.** If he or she takes a morning nap and evening bath, try to keep this routine. Of course, there are times when everyone's schedule will have to change, but do not plan a morning trip to the zoo just to show your former spouse that you don't have to follow the same routine he or she has with the baby. Your former spouse will be upset, but the one you really hurt is your infant.

# EXERCISE 3

*Keeping your children on stable ground*

## FOR PARENTS OF TODDLERS AND PRESCHOOLERS

If your child is a toddler or preschooler think back a year or two about the routine you followed when he or she was a baby. How has it changed? Does he or she still have a security blanket or toy? (Having a security blanket at all of the ages covered in this book is normal.) What routine does your child have now? Write down a general idea of the routine, and put it aside to look at when his or her specific age group is discussed.

## FOR PARENTS OF INFANTS

This chapter was specifically written to help you think about how to create a plan that will help your child know and love both parents while you maintain a secure routine for your infant. The following exercise will help you assess the strengths and problems you might encounter when you try to develop a frequent-contact plan for your infant. On a piece of paper write:

1. *The name and ages of your children.* For this exercise you will be primarily planning for your infant (approximately birth to 12 months). Underline that child's name.

2. *Things we have in our favor for creating a frequent-contact plan.* List all of the ideas you have about what might help you and your former spouse work out a creative plan for your infant.

3. *Obstacles we face in creating a frequent-contact plan.* List potential problems or special circumstances that may make a frequent-contact plan problematic.

4. *What will work for us.* Reviewing all of the strengths and concerns you have identified, write down a specific plan that you think would work.

5. *Now what?* Write one or two sentences of what you will need to do to implement the plan you've developed.

# KEVIN'S EXAMPLE

*Kevin is the 25-year-old father of 4-month-old Stephanie. He and his wife, Rose, have only been separated two months. Rose is living in their apartment, and Kevin is living with his parents.*

**1. Stephanie Mary, 4 months old.**

**2. Things we have in our favor in creating a frequent-contact plan:**

- I want to see Stephanie. I miss her.

- Rose says she wants me to be a part of Stephanie's life.

- I work close to where Rose and Stephanie live. It is possible that once in a while I could even go over on my lunch hour.

- My parents are willing to help me with Stephanie. They can set up a crib at their house.

- Rose's parents are not taking sides. I think they will support any plan that Rose and I agree on.

- There was no violence or drug use involved in our breakup.

- Rose and I used to be able to talk about anything.

**3. Obstacles we face in creating a frequent-contact plan:**

- I get very upset when I see Rose. I still am hoping we can work the marriage out.

- I don't know much about babies. I might feel uncomfortable bathing Stephanie while she is so little.

- Rose is nursing.

- I don't ever want to run into Eric, Rose's boyfriend. I hate him!

**4. What will work for us (maybe?):**

- I could go over to the apartment on my lunch hour on Tuesdays and Thursdays. I could play with Stephanie and hold her before her nap. After I leave, Rose could nurse her and put her to bed. I could even arrange an early lunch, say 11, if that would help. If it is too difficult for Rose and me to be together alone, perhaps our neighbor would be willing to come over. At least we could try this.

- On Saturday, after Stephanie's nap, Rose could bring her over to my parent's house. I could return her to Rose in two hours; I think that is about the time she wants to eat again.

- If Rose does not want me at the apartment during the day, perhaps I could take Stephanie for a stroller walk right after work.

**5. Now what?**

- Ask Rose to go to marriage counseling. If she won't, then try to accept the end of the marriage. Focus on Stephanie.

- Write out this plan. Ask Rose to go to a mediator to help us agree on a plan.

- Learn more about babies. Get a book from the library, or ask Rose to suggest one.

## DISCUSSION

Kevin was devastated when Rose, his wife of four years, told him she had made a mistake marrying him. After their daughter was born, Rose revealed that she had always been in love with Eric, a boyfriend from high school. They had been secretly seeing each other. Kevin was in such despair he could barely go to work. He begged Rose to reconsider, but she steadfastly refused. Finally, hoping to ease the pain he moved home with his parents. Rose filed for divorce. Reading about the needs of infants and doing the exercise helped Kevin focus on Stephanie. He realized that because of the anguish of his loss, he had been forgetting about his relationship with his young daughter. He might not be able to get Rose to go to marriage counseling, but he could work at being a responsible, involved father. Kevin felt a sense of hope for his future when he finished the exercise.

## EXERCISE FOR INFANTS

Take your baby on a nature walk. You can push your child around the block, or just carry him or her around the yard. Point out things, such as, "This is grass. See the kitty. Feel the wind." Your baby will feel interested and happy at the tone of your voice. If your infant is in a stroller, stop occasionally and bend down so you are at eye level, then point out something. Nature walks are helpful for parents, too. When life is in turmoil, just slowing down and looking at the world is soothing. If your baby falls asleep, continue the walk for yourself. Babies like outside walks, even if they are asleep.

## EXERCISE FOR TODDLERS

Take your toddler on a nature walk. Don't plan to walk too far because toddlers' legs get tired. You may want to bring the stroller, just in case. Toddlers are learning that words represent things, such as colors, size, and sounds. They are working at making sense of it all, but they don't have everything figured out yet. You can say, "There's a big dog. The kitty says meow. See the bird. Smell the flower." As with an infant, your toddler will love sharing this adventure with you.

## EXERCISE FOR PRESCHOOLERS

How about a nature walk for the preschooler. You can ask her or him, "Where's the dog? What does the dog say?" Or, "See the red bird; it's making a nest. The nest is the bird's house." Don't put pressure on your child to "know things," just have fun looking at nature.

# CHAPTER 4

# TODDLERS—AN EXPANDING WORLD

> "Robin is such a smart little girl. She talks up a storm and is so aware. But I'm afraid when she goes with Jim for the weekend. She cries when she has to leave me, and I'm worried that Jim will forget she is only 2 and won't really watch her. She's always climbing and getting into things."
>
> —Leah, divorced mother of a toddler

Most toddlers are very adventurous, and they need to be watched to make sure they don't get hurt. They may also cry when they are taken from their normal routine. Leah's fears are normal. But Jim gets defensive about Leah's concerns. He blames Leah for Robin's crying and reports that after about an hour Robin usually settles down.

This divorced family scenario is typical—Mom worried, Dad defensive, and the toddler upset. Not a good atmosphere for anyone. Leah and Jim separated when Robin was 14 months. She lived with both parents throughout her first year. The parenting plan in their divorce decree was a typical boilerplate arrangement, with Jim having Robin every other weekend, Friday to Sunday, and for dinner on Wednesdays. These arrangements may work well for some 8-year-olds, but 2-year-olds have developmental needs that must be taken into account when creating a parenting plan.

# WHO IS THE TODDLER?

There is no definite cutoff point between infants (who in this book have been defined as birth to 14 months old) and toddlers (14 months to 2½) or toddlers and preschoolers (2½ to 5); so in some ways your child may seem more like an infant or a preschooler. As I am using the concept of *toddler,* the three distinguishing features are: 1) increasing mobility (walking and climbing), 2) great strides in talking and learning about the world, and 3) a growing awareness that "I am a separate person"—the terrible 2s!

If you have a toddler, you know that they have a great zest for life because life is full of wonderful surprises and treats. The toddler wants to discover all of them, wants to do it now, and wants to do it his or her own way. Toddlers wear their emotions on their sleeves; they cry or throw tantrums when their plans are interrupted or fail; they love with abundance; they openly respond to environmental stimulation (the love of snow, rain, music, drums). At the end of the day most toddlers are tired, exhausted from their exuberance, but they often resist sleep because they do not want to give up one minute of exciting experiences. The mobility they exhibit and the words they use may lead adults to assume toddlers know, understand, and can do more than they are able. The toddler does not understand complex concepts like *divorce*, *marriage*, *death*. They may even confuse a seemingly simple concept like *dog*, using the word to describe a cat or horse—although, as the child grows, he or she will know and understand increasing categories of animals.

Toddlers do not comprehend time. If you tell a toddler that he or she will get to do something tomorrow, the toddler has no idea whether that means five minutes from now, a month, or after his or her bath. This, of course, presents many problems in helping the child to understand visitation. "When is Daddy coming?" the child asks. The mother replies, "You will see Daddy on Saturday," and points to the day on the calendar. Later in the day the toddler looks out the window, "Where is Daddy?" The mother begins to feel frustrated. This conversation may happen several times a day. Or the child may realize that his or her questions are upsetting the mother (remember the young child is very aware of emotional tones), so he or she doesn't ask. Not asking does not mean the toddler doesn't still wonder.

The toddler may even use words correctly, and the parent assumes that the child understands what he or she is saying. This can create many problems between divorced parents. The child says, "When is Daddy coming?" The mother responds, "Now what did I tell you? Mommy and Daddy are . . . ?" The toddler correctly answers, "Divorced." "That's right! And when will you see Daddy?" "Saturday." "Good, that's right. Now finish your lunch."

In this illustration, the mother assumes that because the toddler gave her the right answers that the child understands. In reality the child knows that her mother is happy with her, that she has preformed well. But she has no understanding of what is going on. She does not understand what *Saturday* and *divorce* mean—all she knows that it has something to do with Daddy and where he is. Parents should not avoid using terms like *divorce*, *tomorrow*, *September*, *weekend*, but rather they must understand that those concepts are beyond the grasp of the toddler. Parents should try to sense what the child is feeling when he or she asks questions. Answer the feeling, but use the words too—this is how children learn language skills.

As with language skills, the emergence of motor skills does not mean the child knows what is dangerous or what he or she can do. The toddler boy may think he can walk to the grocery store two blocks away, but halfway home he tires and wants to be carried. Or the toddler girl may take joy at jumping off of a pier only to find herself in water over her head. The young child does not engage in these unplanned or dangerous events to irritate parents or end up in the hospital. The toddler is impulsive and oriented toward exploration and growing up. The toddler doesn't even know he or she is at risk. *The toddler must always have responsible supervision.*

All children thrive on a dependable routine. The toddler, experiencing so many developmental thrusts, desperately needs routine. Your toddler may resist following a routine, but remember, you are the parent. This does not mean you can't make exceptions, you can and should. All families need to be flexible. However, once a parenting plan has been established, try to set a similar routine for eating and naps at both homes.

## SEPARATION ANXIETY, AN IMPORTANT CONSIDERATION

About 9 or 10 months old (some parents report 7 months), the child begins to realize that he or she is a separate person. The infant also begins to be aware of other people, recognize faces, and knows who the special, safe person is in his or her life. This is the one who tucks in, feeds, cuddles, comes when the baby cries. The child begins to know when this special person is gone and protests her (or his) leaving, for the infant realizes that safety and well-being are related to this person's presence.

Separation anxiety stems from the child's inability to hold on to an image. When a person is gone, he or she doesn't exist. When the child is away from his mother, he can't picture the mother sitting at home waiting for him or her. "She is gone! Where is she?" (This is one of the main reasons for establishing the frequent-contact plan with nonresidential parents. It helps the infant remember the one parent while keeping close to the other.)

Separation anxiety may be a problem for any child between 9 months and 3 years. The stronger the attachment, the more difficult the separation. Thus, a child who has been in day care since infancy may show separation problems when moved to another teacher or when the routine changes. The child is primarily attached to the primary care giver but also feels the security of a teacher and of the routines in life.

What do separation problems look like? When children are separated from the person they are most attached to, they protest and cry. Next they search for the person, look out the window, ask for Mommy or Daddy, go to the door. Finally they feel a kind of despair and are quiet. This is why many parents say, "Oh, he was fine after about an hour." Somewhere between 2½ and 3, most children are able to create an internalized picture of the parent; then, even when they are away from the parent, they know that the parent exists somewhere and they will be with him or her again soon. When children begin to understand aspects of time (closer to age 5 or 6), they will even know when they will see the other parent. Before age 3, most children will experience anxiety and internal fear when they are away from their mothers too long. Of course, what is too long for one child may be just right for another.

## DIVORCE, SEPARATION, AND VISITATION

Potential problems with separation should be taken into account when planning a schedule that allows for both parents to spend time with the toddler. Problems created when parents ignore or do not understand separation anxiety may turn into major areas of conflict between divorced parents with toddlers. There is a tendency for parents to interpret the child's behavior in a way that will prove to them what they want to believe. Many problems between parents have to do with control, each wanting what fits their needs. When a mother worries about her toddler's being carefully watched, the dad protests that the mother is overprotective. If a dad wishes to see his child during the week, the mother says it won't fit with the child's schedule. When a toddler misses Dad or wants to go home to Mom, the other parent may discount the child's feelings.

Accept the reality that most toddlers need to see their primary attachment figure, usually their mother, daily. Young children adjust best if they do not start overnights until they are 2½ to 3. If you divorce when your child is about 2, you should have a two- to three-month transition period that is similar to the infant visitation schedule (frequent, but short contacts in familiar settings). This is to be followed by weekend visits with the nonresidential spouse, say 10 a.m. to 4 on every Saturday or Sunday, and an early dinner one night during the week. The weekend day and weeknight visits should remain constant for six months. Then overnights can be introduced with one overnight a weekend. By the age of 4 the child will probably feel comfortable being away from his mother for a five-day vacation.

If you are the nonresidential parent and want to spend more time with your child, this may seem like a lot of complicated work and feel like a long time before your son or daughter can be with you in the way you want. It doesn't seem fair that your former spouse is having so much time with your child when you know that you are a good, caring parent. In reality it is only a time span of a year or two. Allowing your child time to grow and develop and gradually adjust to being away from his or her primary care giver means you will have a happier child. Attention to your toddler's needs now will help you have a better relationship with him or her over time. The payoff for inconvenience is establishing a positive lifelong relationship with your child.

## TIPS ON TODDLERS

- When you talk on the phone with the other parent within earshot of your children, keep voices calm. Do not quarrel or try to solve issues in front of the children. Remember that they are like little radars, picking up all emotions. If the toddler feels you are okay, then his or her life will feel safe.

- When one parent moves out, let the toddler go to the "new house" as soon as possible (just a short two-hour visit at first). Toddlers like to explore, so he or she will run around, checking everything out. This is what you want.

- At the new house have a box with toys and books that is easy for the child to reach.

- Keep a picture of the nonresidential parent in the child's bedroom.

- Whenever your toddler is going to sleep at the other parent's house, be sure to pack his or her favorite security blanket or toy. Before over-nights begin, this will be for naps. Keep naps at approximately the same time at both homes.

- If you are the visiting parent, don't introduce major parenting changes during your time with your toddler. For example, don't start toilet training your child if your former spouse has not begun this process.

- If you are the residential parent, keep the other parent updated on any schedule changes, health concerns, or new behaviors you are addressing (like toilet training). Don't expect the other parent to do things exactly as you. Close enough is good enough.

- Create a way that you, as parents, can discuss your children in a constructive manner. Some ways that have worked for other parents are a weekly phone call at a scheduled time, meeting at a restaurant every other week, or a monthly meeting with a mediator. In between talk times, you can exchange notes, but do not depend on notes to discuss major issues concerning your toddler or other children.

- If your toddler is in day care, let the day-care personnel know there has been a change in the family. This will help them understand changes in behavior. However, do not use the day-care staff in a war against your former spouse. Remember your child picks up on the feelings of all adults in his environment; it is important for the day-care center to be a safe environment.

- Both parents should know and have access to all health and education personnel (doctors, dentists, teachers). As with the day-care staff, don't involve these professionals in your divorce.

# EXERCISE 4

*Getting past the hurt*

## FOR PARENTS

Divorcing when your child is a toddler means there will be many changes in how you expected to raise your child. For at least 15 to 16 years you will need to co-parent with your former spouse, sharing time and decision making. All parents experience some loss and disillusionment when they divorce, and this is often accompanied by anger and mistrust. For your own peace of mind and for your child's well-being, you must let go of the negative feelings you have toward your former partner. Unfortunately, you can't change the other parent. The only actions or feelings you can change are your own. This exercise is designed to help you look at your attitudes, behaviors, or feelings and determine what you can do to move toward acceptance of the divorce and how you can support the other parent.

On a sheet of paper, write: *Obstacles to a positive post-divorce relationship with* _____ (your former spouse). Under this heading, list all of the major areas of concern (feelings, attitudes, or behaviors) that you have that relate to your former spouse.

Following your list of concerns write: *What I can do to improve our post-divorce relationship*. Under this heading write a response to each of your concerns; remember that you can't change the other parent. Think about what you *can* do.

## NICOLE'S EXAMPLE

*Nicole is the 30-year-old mother of 28-month-old Jonathan and 6-year-old Carla. She and her husband, Ted, have been separated for six months and are in the process of developing a parenting plan.*

**Obstacles to a positive post-divorce relationship with Ted:**

1. Ted has never been very involved with the children. It doesn't seem fair that now, all of a sudden, he wants to be Father of the Year.

2. Jonathan has asthma, and Ted has always felt this was no big deal. I am worried about how Ted will handle an asthma attack.

3. Ted wants to coach Carla's T-ball team. I don't want to have to see him at all of her games. I think he is just doing this to get back at me.

4. Ted was the one who wanted the divorce. Why should he still have all the benefits of a family? I want him to suffer.

**What I can do to improve our post-divorce relationship:**

1. I guess it doesn't matter why he is becoming more involved, the main thing is he does want to spend time with the children. Who cares if he looks like Father of the Year? (I still do care what other people think. I don't want them to think he is a good father! I need to continue to work on this.)

2. Ask, not tell, Ted to make an appointment to see Jonathan's doctor so that she can explain Jonathan's asthma. I have always taken Jonathan to the doctor, so in all fairness Ted may not really understand asthma.

3. It is probably good for Carla to have her dad be her coach. I can run errands during the practices and come back in time to pick her up. I will try not to be angry when I pick her up.

4. It still hurts me to have someone I counted on tell me he no longer wants to be married. I can't believe that at the age of 30 I'm alone with two children. I don't want to go back to work. I don't want to be a single parent. I know I'm bitter. Who wouldn't be? How can I get over this? If Ted suffers, the children suffer. If I suffer, the children suffer. Somehow we must move on. I don't want the children to suffer.

## DISCUSSION

Nicole was painfully honest in completing this exercise. Her anger at being left by Ted is very apparent. During the exercise she began to realize that her anger was probably hampering her ability to start over. She enrolled in a divorce-adjustment group at a local church and is contemplating registering for a course at the community college. The exercise helped her move on a little; it did not solve all of her concerns.

## EXERCISE FOR INFANTS

Gym time! Get out the magic blanket from exercise one. If your baby is very little, take each leg and lift it up. If your baby is learning to sit up, lay the child on his or her back, let him or her hold on to your fingers and pull up. Repeat, being careful to not let the baby fall. If your child is already sitting up, lay the child on his or her back or stomach and help the child roll from side to side. Take the baby's hands and clap. Now just lie on the blanket and watch your baby play. How is he or she playing? The idea behind this exercise is not to begin your little one training for the Olympics, but to touch your baby and stimulate him or her. You may find your child coos and laughs.

## EXERCISE FOR TODDLERS

Toddlers love action. Get a large colorful ball, and pick out a place that is safe—perhaps a basement, a fenced yard, or a kitchen floor. Sit on the ground with the ball and roll it to your toddler. Ask her or him to roll it back. Pretty soon your toddler will catch on and like this game, and he or she will be using developing motor skills.

## EXERCISE FOR PRESCHOOLERS

Let's hop. There are a couple of activities you can do with this fun, hopping exercise. Using colored chalk, draw a row of three or four squares, like hopscotch, on the sidewalk. Make the squares about 20 inches. Then you and your preschooler can jump from square to square, first with feet together, then on one foot. Your child will probably be enchanted with the colored chalk. After you get tired of hopping, let him or her draw in the squares. Put the chalk away for another adventure on another day.

# CHAPTER 5

# PRESCHOOLERS—SO BIG,
# BUT STILL LITTLE

"Tonya says she doesn't want to go with Roger on Fridays. I let her stay home last week, and now Roger is threatening to take me to court if she misses again. I feel so bad sending her off when she is crying."

—Yvonne, mother of 4-year-old Tonya

Roger and Yvonne have only been separated for four months. Roger left the home following an incident that included the police being called after he pushed Yvonne onto the bathroom floor and caused her to cut her forehead. Tonya watched her parents fight and cried for them to stop. Four days after this incident, Yvonne got an order of protection and filed for divorce. For two months Yvonne wouldn't let Roger see Tonya. Finally, Roger's attorney went to court and got an order that stated that Roger could have Tonya every other weekend. Roger had two visits with Tonya before she began crying whenever he arrived to pick her up.

Now both parents are looking at Tonya's behavior as being caused by the other. Roger agrees that Tonya cries when he picks her up, but he says, "If Yvonne wouldn't be so worried about her and would tell Tonya that she is going to have a good time, I know she wouldn't cry. Tonya is fine when she is away from her mother." Yvonne believes Tonya is afraid of her father because of the violence she witnessed.

To understand Tonya's behavior, the parents need to consider the following facts. The first is Tonya's age—she is only 4 years old. Because Yvonne works, Tonya is in day care, away from her mother and her home from 7:30 a.m. until 6 p.m. When Tonya goes with Roger, she really is missing her mother. The fact that she isn't crying at Roger's doesn't mean she isn't feeling sad and lonesome for her mother. The next fact is how the domestic violence affected Tonya. Tonya remembers her mother crying, seeing blood, having the police come to their home. These are scary memories for anyone, but especially for a preschooler. Tonya associates her father with her mother getting hurt. No child wants her mother hurt—not by anyone.

Finally, the parents need to remember that Tonya and Roger used to have a good relationship. Roger would fix her macaroni and cheese, watch cartoons with her, play with her in the yard, and pick her up from day care. Roger is her father, and it is important for Tonya to have a good relationship with him. This young family has been through some bad times. Now, for Tonya's welfare, the parents must be willing to put their own hurts and anger aside and make a plan that will take into account both Tonya's need to see her father and begin to trust him again and her need to spend time with her mother on the weekend. Fortunately for Tonya, Yvonne and Roger were able to meet with a divorce mediator and create a plan that worked toward the goals of establishing a positive relationship between Roger and his daughter while making certain Tonya had enough time with her mother.

## THE PRESCHOOL CHILD

When planning for your child it is important to know your child: What can he or she do? What are his or her interests? What are his or her particular fears and concerns? What is the child's current routine?

Preschool children are older and more capable than toddlers. They verbally express themselves, although not as accurately as an older child. Preschoolers have a memory of books, movies, and events in their lives. They tell their parents about things that happen to them. At this age, children thrive on predictable routines. These routines can be varied, but it is important to keep them as stable as possible. Preschoolers have an ever expanding ability to do things—hop, climb, ride a bike with training wheels, fix a bowl of cereal, talk on the phone.

When preschoolers are away from their parents, they can remember them, understand where Mom and Dad are, and know that they will see them "after work" or "after the birthday party." However, preschoolers usually do not fully understand time. Days of the week mean nothing, so telling a child he will see Daddy on Wednesday does not mean the same thing to the child as it does to the parent. After an hour, the 4-year-old may return to his mother and ask if it is Wednesday yet. Four-year-olds frequently get "yesterday" and "tomorrow" mixed up.

Four- and 5-years-olds want their parents to get along, and if parents divorce the child may begin to keep things to himself rather than say something that will upset a parent. The result is a kind of splitting, where the child will not talk about what goes on when he or she is with the other parent. This is not good for the child, because most preschoolers talk about anything and everything. Of course, if a parent then tries to force the child to talk, it compounds the damage to the child.

## WHAT TO CONSIDER WHEN MAKING A PARENTING PLAN

When parents are building a parenting plan for preschoolers the first thing they must consider is when the divorce took place. If the parents are just divorcing, then the plan should include a transition period where the child can get used to two different families and being away from home. If the parents divorced earlier and have had success with a parenting plan for their toddler or infant, then they may want to move toward a more typical parenting plan where the child can be away from each parent for longer periods of time. Or the parents may be satisfied with the plan they have and decide to keep it in place.

Another important factor to consider is the presence of older siblings. If the preschooler has an older brother or sister, the stress of being away from home is somewhat lessened. The sibling represents the familiarity of home and this helps the preschooler adjust to the change. The presence of a younger sibling is not as protective as the presence of an older sibling. Younger children require much parental attention and care; thus the preschooler may have his or her needs overlooked or may be put in the position of needing to be too grown up. If the preschooler has a younger brother or sister, then planning some time for the older child to be alone with each parent would be helpful.

## SPECIAL CONSIDERATIONS

For some families, like Roger and Yvonne's, special circumstances or concerns must be addressed when creating a parenting plan:

**1. Domestic Violence.** When domestic violence—parents physically or psychologically hurting each other—has taken place in divorcing families it is always damaging to parents and children. The presence of out-of-control behavior may be limited to an incident or two that occurred during the final process of deciding to divorce. Ending a love relationship is very painful—emotions can be intense, and reason and self-control fail. In other families, incidents of domestic violence may have occurred periodically throughout the marriage, and this damaging pattern may be the reason for the divorce. Regardless of why domestic violence occurred or what triggered the incidents, children who have been exposed to violence have been emotionally hurt, and they need special help in healing.

The first consideration in making a plan for the children to spend time with both parents is to make certain all family members are safe. If it has been determined that both parents are safe for the children to be with, the next step is to plan a way to exchange the children so violence will not be triggered. Some parents exchange the children at a neutral relative's home and time the exchange so they avoid encountering each other. Other parents have found they can exchange at a restaurant; still others use a therapist's office or the local police station.

The principle to remember is to use a plan that protects everyone but is the least restrictive. For example, it is better for the children to be exchanged at grandmother's than the police station. However, if the only way to guarantee safety is to use the police department, then that is the choice.

The plan that Roger and Yvonne created was that Roger would see Tonya every Wednesday night for dinner and every Sunday from 11 to 5. On Wednesday night, Roger picked Tonya up at day care and returned her to a neighbor who was a family friend; after he left, Yvonne would walk over and bring Tonya home. On Sunday, Roger picked Tonya up after Sunday school and again returned her to the home of a family friend. The parents agreed to review this plan in six months, and if all was going well to add overnights. The parents were fortunate to have a neighbor who felt comfortable serving this important role. Before the marital separation, Tonya had spent many hours at the neighbor's home with both of her parents, so going to their house did not feel odd or frightening to Tonya.

Tonya was fortunate to have parents who were willing to put her needs ahead of theirs. In the long run, considering her needs enhanced each parent's goal—Tonya will grow up trusting both parents. At first, Roger resisted not having weekends with Tonya, thinking that his friends and co-workers would think he wasn't a fit parent. However, after thinking about Tonya he was willing to try the plan and discovered that he was seeing Tonya more frequently than the judge had ordered. Yvonne's respect for Roger began to be restored as she experienced his willingness to make and follow the new plan.

**2. Substance Abuse.** If there is documented proof of substance abuse such as conviction of driving under the influence, the courts will take it into account when deciding how to guarantee the safety of children. However, parents often express concern about substance abuse but, because there is no proof, it becomes the word of one parent against the other. Seldom will a person with a substance-abuse pattern admit to overindulgence, and seldom will the user understand the precarious position in which parental drinking or drugging places children. Denial of the problem is one of the diagnostic criteria of debilitating substance abuse. This places the non-drug-abusing parent in an ambiguous position. The children need to have a relationship with both parents, yet the substance-abusing parent's behavior could place them in danger. One solution some parents have tried is to create a plan where both parents agree not to drink or use drugs when they are with the children. It must be remembered that such an agreement will not guarantee the safety of the children, because often drug-abusing parents cannot keep their agreement. However, such an agreement does allow the parents to try a controlled nonuse plan. If such a plan works, the children will certainly benefit—first from not being exposed to danger and second from not being exposed to parental conflict over the issue of drug use.

When one parent does not have an addiction problem and only occasionally has a glass of wine or beer, he or she may feel it is unfair to agree to nonuse. The principle to remember is that the parenting plan is not about parental fairness but about the healthy development of the children. If forsaking a glass of wine now and then helps set in place a post-divorce plan that is safe and workable, it is worth the sacrifice.

**3. Chronic or Serious Acute Health Problems.** It is worrisome to parents when their young children have serious health problems. In some instances differences between the parents on how to approach such problems have actually been a factor in triggering the divorce. In other families the management of the child's health becomes a focus of conflict following parental separation.

Two major reasons parents have conflict over health management are that one parent is shut out of decisions or that the parents disagree on the best treatment for their child. In some families one parent, often the mother, has been the parent who assumed primary responsibility for decisions related to the children's health care. The mother took the child to the doctor, saw to it the child took his or her medicine, and so on. Consequently, following parental separation the father is shut out of all knowledge of his child's health care, often not even being informed of appointments or doctor's names. Parents who are shut out become angry, and the child's health care becomes a source of parental conflict. In other families parents genuinely hold different opinions about how to manage the child's health. One parent may believe in minimal drug involvement, applying a get-tough approach to healing, while the other relies on medication and reassuring pampering. These polar positions are usually a result of each parents' past experience, but regardless of how they originated each parent is strongly attached to her or his perspective.

If you find yourself in conflict over your child's health, it is important that you find a way to create a plan where both you and your former spouse cooperate in the health care of your child. Accepting that it is in your child's best interest will help pave the way to working together. Some parents have found that scheduling a consultation appointment for both parents with the treating physician is an important first step. When parents hear together what the doctor is recommending, it is much easier to cooperate. The doctor does not want to get in the middle of a parental battle, however, so do not go to the appointment to argue with the doctor or the other parent. Go to listen and get clarification. If you continue to have disagreements about your child's care, select a new physician who specializes in your child's condition. Have her or him provide you and your former spouse with an opinion and agree to follow this doctor's recommendations for at least one year. An important contribution to your child's health is to reduce all parental conflict.

**4. Other Major Concerns.** Some divorcing parents have concerns about child abuse, both physical and sexual. It is so important to protect children from abuse that if you have any questions, please consult a mental-health professional immediately. If you have limited financial resources, contact your county or state health department, explain your concerns, and ask for a referral to someone who will be able to assess your situation.

*Note:* Although these special concerns appear in the chapter on the preschool child, the issues are equally important to consider when deciding on parental plans for younger children.

# EXERCISE 5

*Laying down plans*

## IF YOU ARE A PARENT WITH AN INFANT OR TODDLER

Reflect on any concerns the discussion on special considerations may have raised for you. Does one of your children have a serious health concern? Was there violence in the home? Are you and your former spouse locked in struggles over personally held beliefs?

If you answered yes to any of these questions, take a few minutes to generate some ways that you and your former spouse can work together instead of working against each other. Take your child out of the conflict. Writing down your ideas will help you work toward a positive solution.

## IF YOU ARE A PARENT OF A PRESCHOOLER AND NEED TO DEVELOP A PLAN TO SHARE TIME WITH THE OTHER PARENT

1. Describe your preschool child, include his or her interests, favorite foods, fears, and so on. Does your child have any special needs?

2. Now write down your preschooler's typical schedule during a day of the week and the weekend.

3. Looking at who your child is and what he or she does, come up with a plan that will allow your child to have as much stability as possible. Write your plan down. Put it aside for a day or two, and then if it still seems like a workable solution share it with the other parent. Keep an open mind!

## MATT'S EXAMPLE

*Matt, 40-year-old father of 3½-year-old Emily and 10-year-old Sean, and Jackie, his wife of 14 years, have decided to seperate and are trying to decide what is best for the children.*

## DESCRIPTION OF EMILY:

Emily is so cute and little. She has short brown hair and big blue eyes. Although she is beginning to thin out, she still has a little baby fat on her arms. Emily is a little bossy; she often tells Sean what to do. Her favorite color is purple—she even has purple tennis shoes. Emily does not like milk, pickles, or Chinese food. Just in the past month she has discovered pizza, plain cheese. She needs at least 10 hours of sleep, and usually goes to bed at about 8 p.m. Emily is afraid of witches and scary noises. Sean can easily scare her by threatening her that a witch will come get her. She loves to go to the petting zoo and wants a bunny. Emily can't wash her own hair yet; Jackie usually helps her. She can dress herself but needs help with buttons. When she has a bad dream, she cries for her mother to comfort her. Jackie is good at reassuring her and getting her back to sleep. Emily likes to go to the hardware store with me.

## EMILY'S TYPICAL DAY:

Emily is up about 7. She comes downstairs for cereal. I leave for work about 7:30. Jackie helps her get dressed, and about 8 they leave to go to the sitter's. Jackie picks Emily up about 4. Emily plays or watches TV when she gets home. I get home at 6. We eat dinner about 6:30. After dinner, I get Emily started in the bath, Jackie cleans the kitchen. Then Jackie finishes up the bath, and one of us reads Emily three books and tucks her in. She is pretty good about going to sleep. I coach Sean's soccer team—we often have games on Saturday. Sometimes Emily comes. I usually work in the yard or play golf on Saturday or Sunday. Emily goes on errands with Jackie. Sometimes we go to my parents' house for Sunday brunch (about once a month). Sean and I like to watch sports on TV. Emily plays around while we are watching TV.

## A PLAN FOR EMILY:

First try to find an apartment near the family house. One night during the week pick up Emily and Sean for dinner. Have them home by 7. This means we will only have an hour. Perhaps one day a week I could leave work a little earlier so I could at least be with her for an hour and a half. Pick her up on Saturday after Sean's game. Have her until 10 on Sunday morning. We will need to have a different schedule for Sean, because he doesn't need to be in bed as early and doesn't need me to wash his hair or get dressed.

## DISCUSSION

Matt was depressed after he looked at Emily's schedule. He realized that with Emily's need to be in bed early, his work schedule, his involvement with Sean, and his own interests that it would be very difficult to spend as much time with Emily as he had hoped. Matt loved having Emily's energetic presence around him, and he felt sad knowing he would not be with her every day. Reviewing his ideas a few days after completing the exercise, Matt shared everything he had written with Jackie. She was touched by Matt's honesty and his desire to develop a plan that would meet Emily's needs. Matt and Jackie decided to try Matt's plan for six months, and change it as Emily got older; they worked out a different plan for Sean so that Matt was able to have more time with him.

## EXERCISE FOR INFANTS

Time to sing! The magic blanket comes out again. (Is your baby beginning to remember this blanket?) Sing a song or two for your infant; don't be shy, even if you don't have a great voice; to your infant you have the most wonderful voice. Don't sing too loud. Loud noises can frighten babies. Use a soft, comforting voice.

Observe your baby, does he or she sing too? That is, does she make little cooing sounds? This is another activity that you can repeat; children love when their parents sing familiar songs.

## EXERCISE FOR TODDLERS

This exercise is designed to help your toddler know that it is psychologically safe to love and miss the other parent. Get a nonbreakable picture frame, such as a travel frame (no glass!), or an inexpensive wallet with places for pictures. Place a picture of the other parent in the holder; if there are more spaces, you can put a picture of yourself, the toddler's pet, and so on. Allow your toddler to carry his or her pictures around, or place the picture holder where the toddler can pick it up whenever he or she wants to see Mommy or Daddy. Remember, your toddler listens to the sound of your voice. Try not to have a harsh or cold tone when you refer to your former spouse.

## EXERCISE FOR PRESCHOOLERS

This exercise is designed to help your preschooler begin to understand and accept that he or she has two family centers, one with Mommy and one with Daddy. Find a small, but not too heavy picture album. Gather together pictures of both parents, the preschooler, other brother and sisters, grandparents, and each home. Sit down with your child and create a section called *Daddy* another *Mommy*. Then put the appropriate pictures in each section. As you work on this project with your child, talk about the family and establish a feeling of trust and acceptance of the current arrangement. This picture album may be added to—or new ones started—as the two families change through remarriage, birth of half-siblings, new homes, or additional pets. This is your child's album. Let the preschooler look at it or carry it around whenever he or she wants.

# CHAPTER 6

# UNUSUAL FAMILY CIRCUMSTANCES

"How am I ever going to know my son?" asked John, who had just learned of a company transfer from Lincoln, Nebraska, to New York City. Luke is John's 15-month-old son; he and his former wife Ellen, have been divorced for three months.

Divorcing parents with young children are often pushed to be flexible and make arrangements that may inconvenience them, keep them apart from their child for extended lengths of time, or stretch financial resources. When an unexpected event occurs, as John and Ellen faced when John was transferred 1,000 miles away, parents need to draw upon their creativity, goodwill, and problem-solving ability to design a plan that will allow their young child to know both parents and take into account the child's developmental needs. Geographic separation is not the only situation that a divorcing family may face. Some parents have never married—and although both parents and children in this situation have legal rights, the parenting roles and couple history are usually not like those of a married couple. In other marriages, a parent may reveal that she or he is homosexual and must leave the marriage. In all of these complicated situations, the parents will need to work together especially hard for the well-being of their children.

# PARENTING ACROSS THE MILES

Ellen was surprised when her former husband John called her at work to tell her that his entire department was being moved to New York City. John and Ellen had become aware of their differences during their first year of marriage. When they mutually agreed to divorce, they did not know Ellen was pregnant. They stayed together during the pregnancy, but when Luke was 6 months old John moved to an apartment nearby and the couple began the divorce process. Their divorce had been final for three months. Luke was into a routine of seeing John three to four times a week. Ellen went to night school and ran errands during the times John was with Luke. It finally seemed that their lives were settling down. Now this!

John was torn. If he didn't move, there would be no job for him with the company. Although he might find another job in Lincoln, it would be almost impossible to match his current salary. John loved adventures, and living in New York City appealed to him; it seemed exciting, busy, and offered opportunity. On the other hand, he couldn't imagine not being able to see his son on a regular basis. Like John, parents usually move away for financial opportunities, although some parents relocate for health reasons or to be near extended family. All of the reasons to relocate are valid, important factors, but the reality is that for the child it will mean lost contact with one parent.

Ellen and John talked over the options and decided that John would take the transfer. Now their task was to make a new plan for how Luke would see his father. The first thing John realized was that he would have to develop a different type of relationship with Luke than the one he would have if he remained in Lincoln. Many move-away parents have difficulty accepting the reality that phone calls and e-mail do not replace person-to-person, day-in, day-out contact. Calls, letters, and cards are certainly important, but they are not Daddy or Mommy. Next, Ellen and John decided that Luke would not fly as an unaccompanied minor until he was 7 or 8, which was six or seven years away.

What to do until then? With the help of a mediator, they decided to make a plan for just one year and at the end of that time assess Luke's adjustment and any changes in their own lives. The first year apart would probably require the most flexibility and commitment by both parents. The next major principle they decided on was that during the first year Luke would not be separated from Ellen except for a few hours at a time. This meant that John would need to fly to Lincoln for visits or Ellen would have to travel to New York with Luke.

Fortunately, for the first six months John would be coming to Lincoln every four to six weeks to follow up on projects. They agreed that when John was in town, Ellen would arrange her schedule to accommodate him. The first evening or two, John would come to Ellen's home, play with Luke, eat with him, let father and son get used to each other again. The third day John would take Luke to his parents' house for several hours but return Luke to Ellen at least an hour before bedtime. This would be repeated every evening. Ellen had a cousin living in New Jersey. She agreed to take a week of her vacation and fly to New Jersey. She would travel with Luke into New York City once, spending at least two hours at John's apartment. John would make at least one trip to New Jersey. Ellen also agreed that once a month she would e-mail John a brief overview of what was going on in Luke's life. John had wanted her to do this weekly, but Ellen felt that that was too much to ask. Ellen was getting tired of so much contact with John—after all, they were divorced! Although neither parent was sure how their plan would work, when John moved they had a sense of hope knowing they had put Luke's needs ahead of their own.

If you find yourself in the position of living far away from your young child, it is important to try to implement some of the same principles Ellen and John used:

- Regardless of geographic separation, a young child needs to have a relationship with both parents.

- Children and parents who do not have frequent physical contact will develop a different relationship from one where children see the parent frequently. An important consideration is that children and parents know when and how the contacts will be and for both parents to support the plan. Children need reliability.

- Very young children should not be taken abruptly from their secure environment.

- Young children need time to feel comfortable with the absent parent. Even when the absent parent has an excellent relationship with the child, the child will need a warm-up time.

- In most cases children under 2 should not be separated from their primary caretaker overnight; children between 2 and 3 should not be away from the primary caretaker for more than two days; children between 3 and 4 can be away for three to four days, and 5-year-olds for five days. (Remember that the presence of older siblings helps younger children feel more secure during separations.)

- Generally, the absent parent should do most of the traveling. This may require making long trips for short contacts. The payoff for this commitment comes as the parent develops a positive relationship with the child.

- The primary caretaker needs to accept responsibility for keeping the absent parent informed about the child's life experiences.

## SOME FINAL THOUGHTS ON GEOGRAPHIC SEPARATION

Some parents, given an option, put off a business-related move until their young child is older. If that is a possibility, it is preferable. Because infants and toddlers have difficulty keeping a person in their memory, the frequent-but-short visitation plan is recommended. Children may be fascinated with the phone, but they certainly cannot get to know a parent through phone calls. If you are going to be separated from your young child, the importance of working on maintaining a relationship with her or him cannot be stressed enough. The years of inconvenience you may have to put up with will be worth it. Your child needs you and needs to know you cared enough to invest time and energy to stay connected. The appreciation of your commitment may not be fully understood by the child until he or she is an adult. Remember as parents we are in it for the long run.

## WE NEVER MARRIED, BUT THERE IS A BABY

Parents who never married are often faced with the same legal stress as divorcing parents. If paternity is established, then the father has the same rights and responsibility as a divorced father—that is, he has a responsibility to financially help support the child and a right to spend time with the child. Thus, the parents find themselves planning schedules and visits, much as divorced parents.

The living circumstances of never-married couples is varied. Some couples have never lived together or made a long-term commitment to each other. When they find they are going to have a baby, the range of emotions include feeling trapped, angry, unaccepting, resigned, or even happy and excited. Some mothers go through pregnancy alone, with no support or interest from the father. Other fathers support the mother through the pregnancy, but remain single in every other way. Some fathers deny paternity. Other parents move in together and try to establish a family arrangement. Each of these responses will affect the relationship the parents have following the birth of their child.

## WE DON'T EVEN KNOW EACH OTHER

When parents haven't lived together and shared life, decision making, and histories, they may have no common ground to begin parenting together. If this describes your situation, it would be helpful for you and your child's other parent to meet once or twice to discuss parenting philosophies, hopes, and goals for your child's future. It is not necessary to agree in these areas, but it is important that you feel as if you know the other parent. If it seems emotionally risky for you to undertake this conversation alone, contact a clinical social worker or psychologist to help facilitate the discussion.

The important thing to remember is that from time to time throughout your child's life you will need to talk to each other as parents. Now is a good time to establish a relationship based on the best interest of your child.

## I'M HOPING WE WILL GET MARRIED, BUT . . .

Many unmarried couples are facing the same emotional concerns that divorcing couples face—the loss of a dream and a desired love relationship. Allow yourself time to mourn for the lost partner, but don't use the baby as an object to win back your lover. Parents need to accept the joys and responsibility of parenting because they are committed to their child, not out of a sense of guilt. If you use guilt as a way to keep a lover you will, in all likelihood, eventually lose the lover and the child will lose a parent.

## HE DOESN'T EVEN KNOW THE BABY, AND NOW SOME JUDGE IS TELLING ME I HAVE TO LET HER VISIT HIM

How upset and angry some mothers are when a judge tells them that the father has a right to see the child. It doesn't seem fair that a man who took no interest in the child for months or years can come back into her life and into the child's life. The mother has managed on her own, or with the help of family and friends, to care for the infant. Now this man, who she feels deserted her and the baby, is demanding his rights. It is fairly easy to understand how the mother feels. But there are two other sides to this picture. First, we do not know why the father was absent. Was he afraid, immature? Did he feel overwhelmed, not knowing how to parent without being married? What is his motivation for coming back into the child's life? The answer to these questions may indicate how the father will parent now.

Second, it is important to consider the child's needs. We know it is important for children to have a relationship with both parents. Of course, an infant is not going to ask about his or her daddy, but infants grow into children who will ask. All children want their parents to be committed to them. If the father will be a dependable, reliable figure in the child's life, then despite the mother's understandable anger and hurt it is beneficial for him to play an active role in the child's life. In planning how to introduce an absent, unknown parent to a child, please read chapters three, four, and five, which cover developmental considerations in making parenting plans. The child will need a period of getting to know the absent parent. The parent who is being introduced should have at least five contacts with the child, preferably with the primary care giver present in the first four. Then the parents can set in place a parenting plan based on the child's age.

*If the absent parent cannot commit to a reliable schedule, he or she should not enter the child's life!* A child should not go through the process of emotionally attaching to a parent who will desert him or her; the child is not a pawn to be used in anger over the court requiring the absent parent to pay child support. Child support is the responsibility of all parents. Pay it, but if you really can't commit to seeing your child following a prearranged plan then don't see the child at all.

## HOMOSEXUALS AS PARENTS

It is not unusual for a homosexual to marry a heterosexual. Many gay and lesbian persons struggle with their sexual preference and hope that by marrying they will put to rest their sexual attraction to others of the same sex. In addition, society does not support a parent being homosexual; and many gay and lesbian persons hope to have children. Therefore, it is reasoned, marrying and starting a family will settle these issues, and all will live happily ever after. Nothing could be further from the truth. Marrying does not change sexual orientation, nor does it solve the difficulties inherent in gay or lesbian parenthood.

People have varying beliefs about the morality of homosexuality: some believe homosexuality is a biological occurrence and there is no moral stigma attached to it since the person has no choice; others believe it is wrong or a sin, often believing that the homosexual has a choice. Regardless of their individual, personal beliefs about homosexuality, however, many divorce judges are harsh in their assessment of homosexuals as parents. For the parent who has decided to declare his or her sexual preference and get a divorce to lead a more honest life, the chance of getting a fair hearing in court is risky. However, two divorced parents can create their own agreement for how they will each spend time with their children. If the parents choose not to make homosexuality an issue, the court will not raise it.

The parents who have gone through this experience and have fared the best are those who decided that in spite of the shocking revelation and the dissolution of the marriage they wanted their children to have a good relationship with both parents. It is amazing how happy children can be when parents work together to solve a problem. There is no question that gay and lesbians can be excellent, caring parents. The only question is, can the heterosexual parent overcome his or her own hurt and rejection to promote mutual parenting?

Remember that a child needs the love and support of both parents. This statement is probably repeated two or three times in every chapter, for it is the core of raising happy children after a divorce. If one parent is gay or lesbian, in time the child will know and will come to understand. We all have things we must understand and accept about our parents. The infant or young child has no cognitive knowledge of what constitutes a "normal" father or mother; what matters to the child is how each parent cares for him or her. Therefore, many of the concerns and worries that may be raised about homosexuality are concerns of adults; the concerns of a child are much simpler. If a gay or lesbian parent forms a caring, paternal or maternal bond with his or her young child, by the time the child is old enough to understand homosexuality the child will know the parent and appreciate that Mom or Dad is, in every respect, a "good parent."

## A FINAL NOTE

In addition to the above three family situations that involve special considerations and challenges for divorcing parents with young children, there are others that will require divorcing parents to make special plans or consider creative options. Children with chronic or life-threatening medical conditions, a parent who deserts the family, or a parent in prison are examples of situations in which divorcing parents have special challenges in planning for the well-being of their young child. The same principles that have been discussed in this chapter may prove useful for any divorcing parent in developing a plan for any unique or unusual situation.

# EXERCISE 6

*Making the best of a difficult situation*

## FOR PARENTS

If you are a divorcing parent planning a future for you and your young child and your situation is different or complicated, you may be feeling overwhelmed.

Let's take a time out! Now is an opportunity to identify the positive factors in your life: personal qualities, life conditions, people, and groups that are assets. This exercise will help you find the strength to be a happy adult and a good parent.

Take out a sheet of paper, and write the following:

1. Briefly describe your situation.

2. List at least two or three responses under each of these categories:

• *My useful qualities*—in rebuilding a life or in parenting;

• *Fortunate situations in my life;*

• *People I can count on;*

• *Helpful groups or organizations.*

3. Read what you have listed in number two. In one word, how do you feel?

### LIZ'S EXAMPLE

*Liz is the 23-year-old mother of Bonnie, 2, and Martin, 5 months, and is separated from Warren.*

**My Situation:**

My husband, soon to be ex-husband, Warren, just told me he is moving to Arizona because there are more job opportunities there. I have not worked since I became pregnant with Bonnie; at that time I worked as a receptionist at a dentist's office. Warren is in construction, sometimes there is a lot of money, sometimes there is nothing. I live in an apartment with the kids and am barely making ends meet. I am considering talking to someone at the public aid office to see whether I qualify for something. Warren has been taking Bonnie to his parents on Sunday, and he sees Martin when he picks up Bonnie. I never seem to get a break from the kids.

**My useful qualities:**

• I'm very organized.

• I'm rather outgoing.

• I don't get sick very often.

• I'm in good shape.

• I like to play with my children.

**Fortunate situations in my life:**

• Warren's parents like me and the children.

• My car is paid for.

• I think my upstairs neighbor may be able to baby-sit
  when I go back to work.

• There are lots of want ads for receptionists in the paper.

• My grandfather said he would give me some money if I need it.

**People I can count on:**

• My mother, even though she lives in Florida.

• Warren's parents and his sister.

• My neighbor Sue.

• My brother and sister-in-law.

• My high school friends Debbie and Kim.

**Helpful groups or organizations:**

• I'm thinking of going back to church.

• Maybe the couple's bowling league we were in.

**Having read all this, I feel:** Excited!

# DISCUSSION

Before Liz did this exercise she was feeling very angry with Warren for moving away. She felt he was running away from his responsibilities to her and the children. She was worried about how she could survive financially. When she looked at the resources she had, which included her ability to get a job and find dependable child care, her whole mood began to change. She and the children would be okay. She wanted Warren to be a responsible, involved father, but she couldn't make him be someone he wasn't. She still had a life and a future.

## EXERCISE FOR INFANTS

Make up a little song about your infant. Mention all the special things about this baby. For example, "I love your cute little toes and your chubby feet. You are so happy and take good naps. Daddy is lucky to have a girl like you." Use whatever tune comes to mind. Singing is an excellent way to communicate with infants.

## EXERCISE FOR TODDLERS

You will need two large pieces of drawing paper and washable markers. Sit on the floor with your toddler. Your job is to draw a picture of your son or daughter; it doesn't need to be elaborate, just colorful. When you are drawing, tell your toddler what you are doing, "I'm drawing your big eyes. This is your smile." You can make a picture of you and your child doing something together or just a portrait of him or her. When you are finished, print your child's name in big, bright colors across the top of the picture and write the date. Children enjoy having someone draw them. In fact, you may find your son or daughter will want you to draw him or her several times; it's helpful to have dates on your masterpieces to give you a history of your artwork together. If you want to do an additional exercise with your toddler, use the suggestion for infants—toddlers and preschoolers also love to hear personalized songs.

## EXERCISE FOR PRESCHOOLERS

Think about your preschooler, what are his or her interests? Does your daughter like such things as jewelry, or is she interested in birds? Is your son really into dinosaurs, or is he a budding artist? After you think about your child's interests, go to a local store that carries small, inexpensive toys. Select a treasure for your child, such as new hair ribbons or colored pencils—something that will reflect your child's interests. Now wrap the gift and put it on the pillow in his or her bedroom. When your child discovers the gift, tell her or him it is a gift for just being who he or she is.

*Note:* Once children get a surprise gift, they usually want more, and who can blame them? But don't encourage materialism and greediness. If your child whines for another special gift, make something special for dinner or let him or her pick out the cereal at the grocery store. There are other ways to be recognized than through a gift.

# CHAPTER 7

# PITFALLS TO AVOID

"I'm not going to pay the child support until Connie proves to me that the money I'm sending is being spent on my son! I don't want to support her and her boyfriend."

—Darryl, father of 3-year-old Chris

Making creative plans for your child's future assumes that both parents, regardless of the anger, sadness, and fear they are experiencing as a result of the divorce, are able to put their feelings aside and work together for the best interests of their children. Unfortunately, this is not always true. Some parents get caught in a vengeful web and try to "prove" in court how they have been wronged and how terrible their spouse is.

This chapter explores the role of the courts in divorce, including the purpose of child support, the dangers of using the court system to vindicate your position, and how losing contact with children is a major loss for both parents and children.

## THE COURT PROCESS

Each state has statutes for the dissolution of marriage that govern divorce and related issues following the divorce. Large counties have specific judges who are assigned to hear only divorce and post-divorce cases. In less populated areas judges may travel from town to town, hearing whatever legal issues are on the docket. Specific state laws vary, although there are similarities between the states. All states have laws that deal with how property will be divided, how child support will be decided, how custody is to be determined, and when the court will allow a parent to move children out of the state.

When parents cannot agree on the division of property, child support, custody, visitation, or removal out of state, the judge will hear the case and make a decision based upon the state statutes. The judge is only interested in hearing facts that relate to the specific issue, and he or she is looking at the case through the lens of the law.

Some divorcing parents are disillusioned with and feel bitter about the legal system. They thought that when they went to court they were going to get to be on the witness stand and tell the judge all of the sad and horrible things their spouses did. They believed the judge would then tell the world how terrible their spouses were and award them everything they wanted. Of course, this is not what happens in court.

Telling your story in court could take hours and hours; the court has limited time. Many of the stories you want to tell the judge have nothing to do with custody or child support, they have to do with your marriage. These stories are important to you, but they are usually not important to the legal process. Many of the things you want to say are not facts but feelings. The legal system is based on facts, and the judge has rules that he or she must follow when deciding what to hear. If you ever get on the witness stand, you can only answer a question your attorney asks, a question your spouse's attorney asks, or a question the judge asks. Much of what you might want to say will never be asked.

After all is said and done, you will get a large bill from your attorney; you must pay for all of the time in court, time spent waiting, time preparing documents, time preparing you for court, time on the phone. Your attorney has a job to do, he or she does not work for free; yet some parents feel that their case or their situation is so important that an attorney should be willing to represent them for the privilege of seeing justice done. This is not how the legal system works; if you can pay for legal representation, you will be required to pay your attorney. If you have no assets, there is usually a county system of legal assistance; however, beware: to qualify you will need to prove you are poor, not just unwilling to dissipate your savings.

The reason for painting such a blunt picture of the legal process is to ensure that you understand what you will go through when you decide to "fight it out in court." Have no fantasy that your trial will be like a TV movie. Be realistic about what going to trial will mean. It will be costly, time consuming, and emotionally exhausting.

As difficult as it may be, some parents find they must to go to trial. They need to guarantee their legal rights, to protect their children, or to have someone decide issues for which there is no compromise. If this is you, face the process realistically; it will help you survive.

## CHILD SUPPORT

Darryl and Connie had only been divorced for three months when he decided to withhold child support. In the divorce decree, Darryl had agreed to pay Connie $360 a month for child support for their son, Chris. This represented about 20 percent of his monthly take-home pay, which was the state guideline. He made the decision not to pay when he learned that Connie was dating one of their mutual friends, Will, and that Will occasionally slept over at Connie's house.

When Darryl failed to pay child support, Connie did not have enough money to pay the rent. She explained to her landlord; he gave her time to get the money, but she was worried and embarrassed. When Darryl came to pick up Chris, he and Connie had several heated arguments in front of their son. Chris saw his mother crying; he heard his father swear at his mother and then angrily screech away in the car.

Both parents contacted their attorneys, and Connie's attorney quickly filed a motion to get the past-due child support. The fees for both attorneys totaled $1,100, which the judge ordered Darryl to pay since he had openly ignored the divorce decree. Now not only did Darryl have to pay the back child support, he had more expenses. More important than the money, his son now cried when he came to pick him up, and the parents destroyed the tenuous relationship they had at the time the original divorce decree was entered.

What are the morals of this not uncommon story?

**1. Child support is important for the stability of the children's security.** Child support is not a punishment. Requiring the nonresidential, or noncustodial, parent to pay child support is based on the principle that both parents have a responsibility to contribute to the financial resources necessary to raise their child.

**2. Child support that has been awarded or agreed to is a legal responsibility and must not be stopped without a hearing and a new order stating that the amount is changed.** The amount of child support is based upon the parent's income. There are situations when a parent loses his or her job or when the current job pays considerably less than the one at the time of the divorce. In these cases, the parent should petition the court for a reduction in child support. Never, never stop paying out of spite or anger.

**3. Child support does not have anything to do with the other parent dating or having a friend sleep over.** You may be upset about your former spouse dating or do not like the new friend sleeping over. If you honestly believe your former spouse's behavior is negatively affecting your child, talk with him or her about your concerns. If that conversation is unsuccessful, consult with your attorney. You may discover that there is very little you can control about your former spouse's private life. Do not stop child support.

**4. Arguing about child support, or any other concern, in front of your child is harmful.** Children cannot stand to hear their parent's fight. Young children do not understand what is going on and feel worried and upset. Parental fighting in front of the child may seriously damage the parent-child relationship. Find other times and places to discuss your differences.

## SOME FINAL THOUGHTS ON CHILD SUPPORT

In reality most—but certainly not all—parents who pay child support are fathers. Fathers often feel bad about this. Not only do they resent having their paychecks diminished; they also want to be viewed as important to their child for reasons other than money. "I am more than a paycheck or a college fund," a dad will say. This is certainly true. The positive involvement of a father in a child's life is valuable to both the child and the father. Both benefit from this contact.

However, taking an active part in a child's development does not mean that it isn't also important to provide a child with as secure a home as possible. A secure home requires money for food, rent, utilities, doctor bills, clothes, and transportation. The parent who is providing the majority of care will encounter many unexpected demands, such as school fees, field trip costs, birthday presents, gym shoes, and special treats, like videos or dinner out. None of these items would be considered extravagant, and most parents want their children to have the experiences their friends are having. Therefore, fathers need to separate their feelings about child support from their need to spend time with their children. Both are important. Paying child support on time, even helping out with extra expenses when possible, will benefit your child. A father who is responsible financially *and* actively participates in his children's lives is a wonderful role model for children to have.

*A word to mothers:* If you receive child support, remember that your attitude toward your child's father is important. Think about how he feels—having money taken from his check every week with absolutely no say in how the money is spent and knowing that he will be paying this money for many years. It can seem overwhelming. This does not negate the fact that as the primary care giver you are faced daily with financial concerns. You are the one who must get the prescriptions filled and pay for day care. But an occasional acknowledgment of your appreciation of his financial participation will go a long way in building a secure financial base for your child.

## LOSING CONTACT

No one knows exactly how many parents lose contact with their children after divorce, but estimates are 45 percent of fathers and 30 percent of mothers who do not have custody of their children eventually lose contact. Patterns and reasons vary. Some noncustodial parents keep contact for a year or two and then fade away; others distance themselves from the time of the separation. A divorced parent may not see his or her children for several years and then suddenly reappear.

Following divorce, why do parents lose contact with their children? Some reasons are:

1. The parent experiences so much personal pain and loss when he or she comes to pick up the child that emotionally it is easier to stay away.

2. The parent was only marginally involved with the children before the divorce, so there is little personal reward to the parent to put in the time and effort it requires to be a noncustodial parent. In these cases the children may have little interest in seeing the parent, since the emotional bond was so weak.

3. The residential, or custodial, parent may be so vindictive and fearful that the children have assimilated these feelings and begin to refuse to visit the other parent.

4. The noncustodial parent remarries and the new spouse wants little to do with children from a former marriage.

5. The court determined that there was some danger to the child in visiting with the noncustodial parent, so visits were terminated until certain behavioral changes were made.

If any of these situations describe you or your former spouse, or if your child is in danger of not having a relationship with the other parent, please get help.

Even a parent in prison can keep contact with a child; he or she can call and write. Perhaps the child will occasionally visit. A child needs to have some knowledge of and relationship with both parents. Of course, contact with the parent needs to be safe. Mentally ill, drug-addicted, or abusive parents should have supervised visits and the visits may need to be time limited, but even in these serious situations children can know their parents.

Professional help is often required when a child has to understand and accept the reality of having a parent with serious problems. If this describes your former spouse, please contact a social worker or psychologist, but do not assume that your child should be sheltered from knowing the other parent. Instead, look for ways to help your child have contact or knowledge, even if it is limited.

If you are a non-custodial parent and are tempted to cut off contact with your child because it is too painful or too much trouble, please reconsider. You, too, may need to talk with a professional mental-health worker to get ideas and encouragement. Do it, your child needs you.

# EXERCISE 7

*Putting problems in perspective*

## FOR PARENTS

If you are contemplating going to court, are withholding child support, or find yourself withdrawing from contact with your children, this exercise is for you. It may be difficult for you to complete. It requires you to be honest with yourself. No one will read your answers—so go ahead and give it a try.

Take out a piece of paper, and across the top write down what you are going to do (go to court, withhold child support, or withdraw contact). Now list all the *positive changes* you hope to accomplish by taking this course of action. Next, list all of the *possible negative consequences* of taking this action.

## ADELE'S EXAMPLE

*Adele is the 24-year-old custodial mother of two children, 4-year-old Daniel and 2-year-old Rebecca, and divorced from Mike.*

I have been contemplating taking Mike back to court to force him to obey the divorce decree. He often picks the children up an hour late, his child support is sometimes ten days late, and Daniel comes home saying that Daddy said Mommy is the one who wouldn't let Daddy live with the family. It was written in our divorce decree that neither of us is to say anything negative about the other. I think Mike is doing all of these things just to get even with me. He wants me to be miserable. My parents have been encouraging me to put Mike in his place.

**Positive Changes I hope to accomplish:**

1. Mike would pick up the children on time.

2. Mike would pay the child support on time.

3. Mike would stop saying negative things about me.

4. Someone besides me would see what a jerk Mike has been.

5. Mike would have to take at least one day off of work, something he hates to do.

6. Mike might learn he can't push me around.

**Possible Negative Consequences:**

1. I would spend several hundred dollars on my lawyer, and Mike would still come late and still get his child support to me a few days late. In fact, he might really begin to enjoy doing these things because he will know how much it bugs me.

2. Mike will probably continue to tell Daniel and Rebecca whatever he wants; he might just start telling them not to tell Mommy. That would be worse.

3. As much as I want someone else to see what a jerk Mike can be, it makes me feel immature to have this as a goal. Ditto with number five. I don't want to continue our petty bickering, and going to court certainly would continue the fighting.

4. Mike always has to push the limits. Going to court will probably make him happy. I'm sure he wants to keep the conflict going.

# DISCUSSION

Adele and Mike had been divorced about a year. The divorce was painful for both of them, and Mike continued to blame Adele for the breakup. Adele's parents disliked how he was treating Adele, and every time she mentioned one of his indiscretions they urged her to go to court to show him. Doing this exercise helped Adele realize that Mike would probably never change and taking him to court wouldn't make a difference. As obvious as this seems, it was a revelation to Adele. She had always thought someone could make Mike change.

Next, Adele realized that Mike did come to pick up the children, even though he was often late. And he did pay child support, also a little late. She decided to overlook this behavior. If it got worse, she thought that requesting mediation might be better than court.

Finally, Adele decided not to complain to her parents about everything. She wanted to think about a positive future. This was going to be a hard habit to break, but she was going to work on it.

Following a divorce, it is not uncommon to want to change the other person—to make him or her see the light. It is a major shift when you realize you have no way to make the other person change; in fact, if he or she could change, it probably would have happened before the marriage broke up. The only power you have is to focus on the positive things you can do for yourself and your children.

# EXERCISE FOR INFANTS

Babies love bright colors and having bright objects around them is good for their brain development. Pick three objects in your home: one yellow, one red, one blue. Be sure the objects are safe. It could be a yellow flower, a blue plastic bowel, and a red block. Now show each item to your infant: "See the yellow flower" and so on.

When you have gone through each item, line them up where the baby can look at them. Tomorrow do the same thing. Continue the color exercise for one week.

# EXERCISE FOR TODDLERS

Build something with your toddler. Get out unbreakable household items, such as rolls of toilet paper or paper towels, tissue boxes, or cans of soup. Sit on the kitchen floor and build a town or a castle.

Your toddler will laugh when things fall down.

# EXERCISE FOR PRESCHOOLERS

This age child loves action. Does your child have a tricycle or other toy he or she can ride? If it is warm enough, go outside and let your child ride around. Comment on what a big girl or boy he is. Watch him or her play. Children like playing with their parents watching.

Watching your child also allows you to let go of some of your other tasks and worries for a while. It allows you to see the world through your child's eyes.

# CHAPTER 8

# GRANDPARENTS, AUNTS, UNCLES, AND ADULT FRIENDS

"I don't know what I would have done without my parents. They let me move back home with Nick and Louise. Mother watches the kids when I work three days a week. Without their help I don't know how we would have made it. Still, I'm looking forward to the time when I can afford to be on my own."

—Gwen, 25-year-old divorced mother of two

Gwen's observations capture the experiences and feelings of many divorced parents with young children. Divorcing at a young age, early in the life of a new family, often means there is not enough money for both the mother and father to live independently and pay for out-of-home day care. It is not uncommon for the mother to return to her parents' home with her young children and for the father to move in with his parents or grown siblings; this arrangement gives them time to reorganize emotionally and financially.

As helpful as this arrangement is, problems and tensions can arise for both the grandparents and their returning adult children. If you are living with your parents or depending on them for financial support, being aware of potential problems may help you develop strategies to avoid conflicts.

# GRANDPARENTS HELPING
# THEIR CHILDREN AND GRANDCHILDREN

Gwen's parent's four-bedroom home is on a quiet, tree-lined, suburban street. Gwen's family moved into this house when she was in third grade; she attended the local high school and the community college for two years. At the age of 20 she married Paul. Her parents wanted Gwen to finish college; they liked Paul, but they felt Gwen should complete her education. Gwen moved from her parents home to an apartment with Paul. A year after their marriage, Nick was born; 14 months later, Louise came. Paul and Gwen had their hands full—as it turned out, too full; the stress of trying to cope with two young children with limited financial resources developed into constant tension and arguments between the young parents. They divorced when Louise was 9 months old. Both Gwen and Paul moved home with their parents.

Grandparents and other relatives are often the first resource divorcing parents turn to. And this is totally appropriate. These are some ways grandparents may help the divorcing family:

**1. Financially.** The grandparents may pay for an attorney, pick up doctor's bills, buy needed cloths, or fund an adult son or daughter's needed education or training.

**2. Housing.** Allowing the adult child to move home, with or without children, often gives the divorcing parents time to save money and plan for the future. The grandparents' home is often nicer and "more settled" than the parent could afford on his or her own.

**3. Help with the children.** Some grandparents become the primary child-care provider, watching young children while the parents work, go to court, attend classes, or date. Grandparents can also give the single parent respite when a child is sick.

**4. Emotional support.** Even when we are adults, our parents are often our biggest supporters. In a divorce the grandparents often provide encouragement, listen to the struggles, or make helpful suggestions.

Some grandparents support their divorcing adult children in all of the above areas, others in just one or two. For example, if the grandparents live far away, they will not be able to provide child care, but they may be phone buddies and encourage their child or send extra money from time to time. The grandparents may live in a small apartment or home with no room for children to move in; however, they will come to the mother's home to watch the children. Families usually do what they can to help one another. Grandchildren, the young ones we are discussing in this book, benefit when they are nurtured and loved by grandparents, and they benefit when their parents are given enough assistance to function as parents.

# POTENTIAL GRANDPARENT PROBLEMS

During and following a divorce, grandparents may unwittingly create problems. This section is written as much for grandparents as for their adult children. Most grandparents don't want to cause problems. If they know what type of situations to avoid, they will. Problems may come up when:

**1. The two sets of grandparents become competitive,** with each one trying to be the most influential or most important to the grandchildren. This can happen when the families are very different with strong beliefs about child rearing, money, religion, or ways to celebrate holidays. The grandparents may feel that they cannot tolerate their grandchildren not growing up exactly as they envision.

**2. The grandparents become so emotionally involved that, in essence, it becomes their divorce.** In these situations the grandparents tell their adult child what to feel and what to do. "I don't understand what's wrong with you, if I were you . . . ." Grandparents often do have good ideas and suggestions, but these must be offered as suggestions, not as the only possible solution.

**3. One set of grandparents are supportive of their adult child, but the other grandparents are absent,** either through death or lack of interest. The divorcing parent who has no extended family support may get angry when he or she sees the other parent receiving love and help—it seems so unfair. This situation is not the fault of the supportive grandparents, but the divorcing parents may quarrel over such support.

**4. The grandparents take on too much child care,** which results in their feeling tired and overwhelmed. Once they have assumed this responsibility, they do not know how to tell their adult child that it is too much.

**5. The grandparents feel that because they have provided financial and housing support, they have the right to make decisions for their adult child.** When an adult lives in someone else's home, the home owner certainly has the right to establish rules and responsibilities, but they do not have the right to make life decisions. It is often difficult for grandparents to see their children as adults after having had years of being in charge. Everyone needs to learn new roles.

The families that have developed the best post-divorce relationships are those whose grandparents have supported their adult child throughout the divorce but continue to acknowledge the importance of the other parent to the children. They are the grandparents who understand that their grandchildren can love them and love their other grandparents. They discuss concerns and problems with their adult child, but they do not tell him or her what to do. When money or time is given, it is given freely, not with strings attached. Does this seem too idealistic? It isn't. It is a goal worth working toward.

## AUNTS, UNCLES, COUSINS

In some families, adult siblings of the divorcing parents provide some of the same functions as grandparents by providing financial, emotional, housing, or child care support. Much of the above discussion could apply to those families where the adult parent moves in with a sibling. It is important for the parent to remain the adult in charge of the child, even though the aunt or uncle can be very supportive. More often, adult siblings are less involved in the actual day-to-day functioning of their divorcing sister or brother. Sometimes they don't know what type of support to give—how much to say, how to help. Some just want to stay away; they are overwhelmed by what the divorce is doing to their brother or sister and don't even want to know what is going on.

If there are things you want from your brother or sister, just ask. Siblings may not be able to give you what you want, but if you don't ask you'll never know. Some of the support they may be able to give includes occasionally baby-sitting so you can have some free time; accompanying you to court; giving you a ride to the doctor's when your child is sick; picking up groceries when you can't get out; coming over for a cup of coffee or glass of wine; or renting a movie on Saturday night when you are alone. If you find your brother or sister is saying too many negative things, such as running down your former spouse in front of your child, just ask him or her not to do this. You can explain that it will hurt your child to hear bad things about his or her father or mother. Remember that even young children will pick up on feelings and tones. It's better not to talk about any divorce-related issues when the children are around.


## FRIENDS

When going through your divorce, you need adults who care for you, who are interested in your future. You need someone to talk to, someone to have fun with, someone to be interested in your welfare. These important adults may be your parents or brothers and sisters, but during a divorce friends are often an important and wonderful source of support. Throughout this book the focus has been on what is best for your child. Sometimes you may want to scream, "What about my feelings? What about me? I'm sick of always trying to do what is best for my child. I have needs too!" It is natural that you experience intense feelings (anger, happiness, sorrow, fear). When the children are involved, your adult reactions are not to be ignored; they just need to be separated from decisions about the children.

What to do with you? Where can you be furious, brokenhearted, scared? With trusted friends. Friends come in different sizes and temperaments, so a friend who may be willing to watch your baby when you go for a job interview may not be the best person to call at midnight when you are in a panic about court tomorrow. Think about whom you know, whom you like, whom you trust. Make a mental note of who is the best person to talk to about specific concerns. A divorce is a high-stress life change, and the process of divorce and the period of adjustment may take two or three years. There is a danger of burning your friends out. After a while they may not know what to say or may tire of hearing the war stories of infidelity, attorneys, and unfairness. Friendship is a two-way street, so your friends will need you to be interested in them and their lives too—even when their lives seem safe and predictable.

When parents with young children divorce, their children are often around when they do things with adult friends: a girlfriend and her children come over for dinner, a buddy stops by to watch the football game, two single parents take their children to the zoo together. Or the telephone, close at hand, serves as contact to the outside world. As a mother watches her toddler play, she may talk to her friend about the events of the day. These contacts with friends help the divorcing parent stay connected with others; they are necessary. The divorcing parent finally has a friendly ear when he or she needs to unload about the other parent, the other attorney, or just the frustration with everything.

But there is a down side to these friendly chats if the children are present and listening. It is hurtful for children to be exposed to these adult feelings. They feel worried, upset, and scared when they hear their parents express strong negative feelings. Remember young children do not always know what the words and concepts mean, but they do know what your feelings are. By 2½ or 3 the child will fully understand when you are denigrating the other parent. One way out of this dilemma is to have a friend whom you can call after your children are asleep. Be sure they are asleep, for children often listen when their parents think they are asleep. Or you can plan to do something away from the children—go out to dinner, meet for coffee, go work out. Then, with no little ears around, you and your friend can talk freely. Do you have a friend at work? Perhaps you can borrow a lunch hour now and then to talk through your concerns. *The principles to remember are: don't overburden your friends and don't expose your children to strong negative emotions.*

## A WORD OF CAUTION

As helpful and necessary as good friends are, there are times when friends (and grandparents and adult siblings) may actually make a divorce worse by becoming too involved. If you are trying to maintain a level of integrity and decency throughout the divorce, you may be taking a very different approach from a friend who thinks you should "take a hard line," "win" in court, get an attorney who will "take him to the cleaners" or "get custody" for you. Friends have their reasons for these positions. Perhaps they never liked your husband; perhaps they think all women are out to get men; perhaps they went through their own divorces; perhaps they just like a good fight; perhaps they don't really understand legal criteria; perhaps . . . perhaps . . . perhaps. There are always reasons for friends to try to take over the divorce. If you think this is happening, talk to a mental-health professional or member of the clergy to help you sort through what it is you believe and want. You have small children and will need to have a relationship with your former spouse for many years. What is best for you and them?

Finally, as wonderful and important as friends are, consider joining an adult divorce-support group. These groups are held in churches, community centers, and private homes. Ask your attorney or clergy member whether they have any recommendations. The advantage of participating in a support group is that all of the members are concerned with the same issues, share resources, and listen to each other. Sharing concerns in a group like this actually allows you to remain a good friend to your friends. They feel less burdened; you feel less dependent.

# EXERCISE 8

*Appreciating the gifts you've been given*

## FOR PARENTS

If your parents, siblings, friends have been kind and supportive, let them know you appreciate them. Get some crayons and paper and make handmade thank-you notes. Adults like getting handmade notes from little children, but they also like handmade cards from other grown-ups. Mail your cards so they arrive as a great surprise.

## EXERCISE FOR INFANTS

It's time for a home exploration. Take your infant into the kitchen. Walk around and point out four or five things of interest, such as, "This is the refrigerator. We keep all of your food cold in here. The refrigerator is white." Then go to the sink and turn on the water, "This is the sink with water for our dishes and ice. At the sink we can turn the water off and on." You can do one or two rooms, and you will find that this is another exercise the baby will enjoy over and over. He or she will not understand what your words are saying but will enjoy the adventurous manner. This helps a child develop wonder and excitement about the world around him or her.

## EXERCISE FOR TODDLERS

If one of your parents or a friend has been especially helpful to you by watching your toddler, let your toddler plan a picnic lunch for that person. Make sandwiches, have pieces of fruit, and cookies. Your toddler can put each person's lunch in a sack, and then later he or she can pass them out. Have the picnic on the floor of the family room, on the front steps, at grandma's, or in the park. Any place is fine as long as there is room for the toddler to run around after eating. This exercise will allow your toddler to help in a grown-up way. It is also modeling doing something special for someone else, an essential quality to develop.

## EXERCISE FOR PRESCHOOLERS

If your preschooler has had an exciting day at preschool, or seen an enjoyable movie, or just fell down and hurt his or her knee, suggest a call to Grandmother or

Grandfather or some other close family friend to tell of the adventure. Write out the phone number in large numbers. Show your child how to dial. Then let the child take over and do the talking. (Some 5-year-olds can push the correct numbers, but they usually need an adult helping.) Children feel grown-up when they talk on the phone. The conversations may not be very long, but they will show your children that there are adults who love them, adults who like to hear about the little things in their lives. If you and your former spouse have a congenial relationship, you could have your preschooler call the other parent from time to time. The qualifier "congenial" is necessary because some divorced parents look on the child calling as a way for their former spouse to keep track of them. Sad, but true.

# CHAPTER 9

# DATING AND REMARRIAGE

"We used to get along great, but ever since Jeff remarried there have been big problems. I think that Monica—that's his new wife—is jealous or something. She's never had children, and I get the feeling she's pretending that Tracy is hers. Maybe I'm wrong."

—Joanne, divorced mother of 3-year-old Tracy

Divorce introduces the first of many changes and adjustments you will be required to make. Joanne and Jeff divorced when their daughter was almost 2. They spent several hours meeting with a divorce mediator to develop a parenting plan for Tracy. It seemed perfect; both parents were satisfied, and even more important Tracy seemed well adjusted. Just a little over a year later, Jeff remarried; that was six months ago and now everything is up for grabs. Tracy complains about going to visit Jeff. She tells Joanne that Monica won't let her sleep with her favorite blanket or wear her patent-leather shoes and that Daddy and Monica won't let her come into their bed when she's afraid of bad dreams. Tracy cries when Jeff comes, clinging to Joanne's legs. Jeff is certain that in some way Joanne is putting Tracy up to this behavior; he thinks that perhaps Joanne is upset that he remarried.

What is happening here? Who is jealous of whom? And how can the parenting routine stabilize again so that every visit will not upset Tracy? Let's start at the beginning. Let's start with dating.

## STARTING OVER

The odds are that at sometime, somewhere, someplace you will meet another person whom you are crazy about. You may begin to think that you can have the family life you hoped for when you first married. The typical professional advice is: don't marry the first person you date, be on your own for at least one year after the divorce, learn that you can take care of yourself and your child, give your child plenty of time to get used to the new person in your life, introduce new people slowly and carefully. These words of warning are all sound, and if followed the chance of a second marriage succeeding is enhanced. But people live their lives the way they want, and from time to time we all make illogical decisions.

All of this is a prologue for some advice on dating. Use what fits.

**1. Dating (and later marrying) someone you were involved with prior to the divorce.** This scenario—the affair that turns legitimate—probably has the most obstacles to overcome. If while you were married your spouse became aware of the affair, it is going to be difficult for him or her to ever get over feeling betrayed. There are some steps you can take that may help.

First, apologize to your spouse for the deception. This does not mean that you believe the marriage is salvageable, but it will convey that there was a better, more honest way to have ended the marriage. Don't apologize if you don't mean it; compounding dishonesty will not begin to build a foundation of trust. Parents, even divorced parents, need to be able to trust each other. After all, at times each of you are solely responsible for the well-being of your children.

Second, when you have the children do not include your new partner in any activities until several months after the divorce is over. This advice is often not followed. Take a minute to think about this; what does insisting that a new person be welcomed into their lives say to your children? It puts the children in second place in importance.

Usually there is plenty of time for you and your new love to spend together when the children are not around. If your girlfriend or boyfriend won't honor your decision, then how willing is she or he going to be when other sacrifices will need to be made for your children? After the divorce is finalized, you can begin to introduce your new friend to your child gradually; an afternoon here, a dinner there. After two to three months everyone may feel comfortable spending considerable time together. If you follow this plan, you will have the best chance of reestablishing a trusting relationship with your former spouse. It's worth a try.

**2. Introducing your child to your dates.** Just meeting a friend now and then will usually not cause any problems for a young child, if meeting really means just meeting. Children meet their parents' friends all of the time, to them a friend is a playmate. But don't overinvolve your young child if the dating relationship is still in the exploratory stage. Your child already has gone through a number of changes and adjustments; take time getting to know someone before you expect your child to emotionally invest in a new person.

**3. Involving your new love interest in the parenting of your young child.** This is a difficult situation. Many women are drawn maternally to an infant or young child, and under similar circumstances a man responds as the protector and wise one. It seems instinctive. Therefore, when you are at the zoo with your new girl-friend, she may wash your 2-year-old's face and offer to change her diapers. Your new boyfriend may tell your 5-year-old not to hit his brother or may show him how to pedal a new bike. It is fine when someone you date pitches in, helping with an extra pair of hands or making some suggestions. The question you need to ask yourself is, "Am I looking to this person to take care of me and my child?" Your child has two parents; new love interests, and later new spouses, can be positive influences in your child's life, but you must always function as the parent. Being the parent means that your ideas and values will be shared with your child, along with your former spouse's ideas and values. Your developing child will integrate all of his or her life experiences and in the end create an individual identity. Your child wants to know who you are. Nice girlfriends and fun boyfriends are okay, but you need to parent your child.

A single parent needs adult time—time to go out and date—but occasionally has no one to baby-sit, so the parent includes the child on dates or has dates over to the house when the child is around. It is difficult to find dependable, safe, affordable baby-sitters. But rather than expecting an infant or toddler to keep late hours or be overlooked while adults try to get to know each other, look harder for a safe sitter. Call a nearby church, explain your situation. There may be a volunteer grandmother that would be willing to give you a break once a month. Or call the YWCA; they have many resources for women and children. Whatever you do, don't leave your young child alone at night with a sitter who is under 14; during the day, for a short time, a mature 12-year-old can sit.

A final thought: Have fun! Love again!

## REMARRIAGE, A NEW FRONTIER

Most parents reading this book will get married again; in fact, some will already be remarried and are reading this book in hopes of finding suggestions that will help in yet another transition for their young child. Jeff and Joanne's experience, outlined at the beginning of this chapter, is not unusual. Stable, post-divorce routines are often upset when one of the parents remarry. Let's examine why problems may occur and look for ways of avoiding potential pitfalls.

**1. One or both of the divorced parents have not let go of the marital relationship.** A person's connection and attachment to a spouse is usually very strong. It takes time to learn new ways of relating to a former spouse—time to let go of the marital bond yet keep the parental bond. The parties must learn how to view the other as an important asset for the children but not a partner for themselves. Even in extreme cases, where there has been severe domestic violence, drug use, or overt infidelity, the parties may have a bond. When one partner remarries, it publicly signifies the ending of the special relationship that once existed and establishes that another person is now in the role of intimate adult companion. Reactions vary from extreme sadness to anger and may be demonstrated by a new rigidity or lack of communication around the children. Of course, this only hurts the children, because they feel the change in the parental relationship.

If you feel hurt or angry because your former spouse remarried (often though you are remarried yourself), admit it to yourself. This is the first step in accepting life as it now is. Next, talk to a neutral third party, such as a mental-health professional or member of the clergy. Ask for help.

In some remarriages the former marital partners have accepted the dissolution of their marriage and have already made the transition to a parenting relationship. Only you know where you are in the process.

**2. The newly remarried family wants to establish itself as a family, which is difficult when the children are members of two families.** We all have an ideal, a picture of what a family is; this picture is usually composed of a mother and father and children born to or adopted by the married couple who all have the same last name and all live together. When newly remarried families form, the newlyweds may have an ideal of the "typical" family in mind, even though they know that there are ready-made children who have a mother or father somewhere else and that the children are not under their control or influence all of the time. If the partners in the remarriage are flexible and have the ability to live in an ambiguous situation, there may be few problems for the children. But if one or both partners attempts to build a family just like the family of their dreams, there are bound to be problems. It is estimated that it takes healthy, well-functioning remarried families at least three years to adjust to the new structure. You need to know this! Getting remarried and establishing a new family is difficult, and you must be willing to have your children be influenced by and spend time with a very important person not in your new family, namely your former spouse. It can't be all your way, no matter how right or justified you feel.

If you or your spouse remarries someone who has never been married or who has never had children, the process may be more difficult, for the new partner may envision herself or himself as moving into a parental role. Any reminder that another person is part of the children's life is felt as a threat. The children hear such things as, "Your mother doesn't wash your hair often enough." "Your father is too strict." "Why does she let you stay up so late?" "How can he expect you to be healthy if you don't have vegetables at least once a day?" And on and on. Even a 2-year-old knows that the stepparent is saying something bad about Mommy or Daddy. Not a good way to begin establishing a smooth parenting relationship.

Another common battle is what the children are to call the new partner. Little children often call any person who is acting in the role of parent either Mommy or Daddy. It doesn't seem to them that this is being disloyal to their mother or father; they know who their parent is. Adults go crazy when they hear their treasured child refer to someone else as *Daddy* or *Mommy*. It is best not to get upset and accuse the other family of undermining you. Just say something like, "Oh, you mean John?" and let it go. Sometimes don't even say the given name, just overlook it. By the time your child is 8 or 9, he or she will probably always refer to the stepparent by his or her given name. If you make a big deal of it now, it confuses and upsets your child. Ideally the stepparents and divorced parents will be able to communicate and cooperate about issues relating to the children. Sometimes a session or two with a therapist or mediator helps establish new rules and ways of communicating. If you are having problems, this may be something to consider.

## ANOTHER LOOK AT REMARRIAGE

Remarriages can be hard work, but sharing life with another adult is wonderfully rewarding. So even though you should be mindful of potential problems, don't be discouraged. A new partner for either you or your former spouse will share many of the growing-up years with your child. The stepparent can be very important in the life of your child. And it will be helpful for you to have another adult to pitch in with all of the tasks that need to be done. Discussing child rearing with another caring adult is also an important role of a new partner. Enjoy your new love and new hope. But be realistic.

# EXERCISE 9

*Bridging the new chasms*

## FOR PARENTS

*If you are dating someone, complete the following brief survey:*

1. Am I spending significant time with my child alone, without my dating companion?

2. Am I depending on my new love to make most of the decisions about what we do with my child?

3. Does my new romantic interest feel I spend too much time with my child?

4. Does my new romantic interest resent it when I have to talk with my former spouse?

5. Have I mastered living on my own?

These are questions to ponder. Take time to look at yourself, your child, and your current situation honestly.


*If you are remarried, complete the following brief survey:*

1. Does your new spouse resent your former husband or wife?

2. Do you and your former spouse establish the primary rules and parenting guidelines for your child?

3. Has it been difficult for either you or your former spouse to let go of the past marital relationship?

4. Are either you or your new partner criticizing your former partner in front of your small children?

5. Are you a flexible person?

Perhaps you and your new spouse might want to sit down and talk over some of the ideas generated by these questions.

# FOR INFANTS

Do you have any bells around the house (maybe from the holidays)? If not, get a spoon, pan, glass, or bowl. Now get out the magic blanket and have "sound time." Ring the bells, tap the glass, pan, or bowl with the spoon. Don't be too loud, remember babies are frightened by loud noises. Repeat the sounds several times. Indulge in the temptation to sing along.

# FOR TODDLERS

What is your toddler's favorite toy or favorite thing to do? Take 15 minutes and play with your toddler. Get down on the floor, follow his or her pace. Your child will love your really being involved at this level.

# FOR PRESCHOOLERS

Popcorn night! After dinner or after nap, make a batch of popcorn. Let your preschooler help in any way that is safe. After the popcorn is popped, put some in a plastic bowl or sack and watch a movie with your child. Don't do grown-up things while you are watching, just be with your child.

# CHAPTER 10

# YOUR CHILD'S FUTURE

"When's Daddy coming home?"

—4-year-old Andy to his mother, Pam

Pam and Norman divorced when Andy was 2. They had an amicable divorce. Each parent wanted Andy to have a good future, and they wanted to minimize the effect of the divorce on his development. Working carefully with a mediator, they created a plan where Norman saw Andy four days out of seven for the first year. They slowly introduced overnights when Andy was 3. There was never any open conflict in front of Andy. All in all, the parents would get an A+ for the way they handled their divorce.

That's why Pam was shocked when Andy returned from two days with Norman and in a sad voice asked her when Daddy was coming home. She thought he understood divorce, that he was well-adjusted. Pam was right to some extent; she and Norman had done everything they could to make the change in their family as easy as possible on their son. Yet despite everything they had done Andy, like all children whose parents divorce, will have to adjust, process, and re-understand the divorce over and over throughout his life.

Andy is lucky because his parents are invested in helping him grow into a child who is not hampered or traumatized by divorce. Andy's life will be different, but not necessarily worse, because his parents divorced.

All parents have a lifetime task raising children. Even when your children are grown, even when you are dead, you will remain their parent. What you do, who you are, how you have invested in them will always be important. Of course, the task will get easier. Parents with young children have the most hands-on work. By 5 many children can dress themselves, some can tie shoes, all can pick up toys. By 10 they can help with the dishes, walk the dog, read silently, and run the VCR. By 16 they can drive! And by 22 they should be able to live as single adults and support themselves. So, during the next few years you will work yourself out of a job; but you can never not be a parent.

Think about the areas of life in which all adults need to function. How could parental divorce affect your child's future? What can you do to help your child step into adulthood, ready to take care of himself or herself and ready to give to others?

## WORKER

One primary adult role is that of worker. While adult work is not an immediate concern for young children, their attitudes toward work are being formed at this early age. Your preschooler may pretend he is Mommy or Daddy and wear your shoes, pick up your briefcase, and get ready to go to work.

All healthy adult people are engaged in some form of work. Some people refer to their work as a career; this usually means that they have made an emotional commitment to their type of work. In addition to the time spent on the job, they invest additional time and energy learning about and pursuing their careers. In past decades it has usually been men who made a commitment to a career in addition to their family, although there have always been women who have pursued careers outside the home. Women who stay home to raise the children and create a family environment often made a "career commitment" to this role. People who have careers are certainly interested in the amount of money to be earned, but they also receive emotional satisfaction from their work.

Other adults view their work as a job or occupation. They perform the tasks needed to be successful, but do not have an emotional commitment to work. If another job that pays more but uses completely different skills becomes available, they can easily switch jobs. People who view work this way may go home feeling some anxiety or worry, but they seldom invest emotional time and energy into work development. If they advance on the job—and many do—it is because they work very well and get great satisfaction from doing high-quality work.

Virtually everyone works partially to make the money needed to survive and prosper. In this sense, all work is partially mere toil. However, most people want to see their work as providing a necessary or useful service or product. Most people will experience their adult work as having some qualities of a job and some of a career. The critical dimension of any adult work is for the individual engaged in the work to feel satisfied and generally happy with what he or she is doing.

Your current attitude toward your work may influence your children's view of adult options. If you feel angry or cheated at having to work outside the home or feel trapped in a particular job because of child-support payments, child-care arrangements, or even the need to live near your children, you may be communicating this to them. When a parent is unhappy with his or her work, the message communicated to the children is, "Adult work is miserable." To help each child develop a positive future, spend the time and energy in creating an adult work role for yourself that is as personally rewarding as possible. If your children view you as generally happy with your work, it will provide them with an adult model that says, "Adult work is satisfying."

Another way you can help your children develop a positive attitude toward adult work is to expose them to the many different jobs people perform. You know your child; as he or she grows and develops interests and abilities, point out the type of work that requires your child's attributes. Encourage your child to try new experiences and master new skills.

The final choice of adult work must be each person's, of course. Do not force a child into your mold but rather encourage him or her to find the right path for himself or herself. All children need encouragement from their parents to explore many options.

Right now you are facing all of the problems of being a single parent of a young child. Career options and graduate school for yourself may seem irrelevant. But are they really? Remember that all healthy adults work at something. You might as well try to work at something you enjoy. This could be the perfect time to think seriously about your own future. If you don't feel good enough about your skills or your job, take time to talk with a counselor and get some guidance. Most community colleges will be able to help you decide an area that seems to fit you.

Many fathers and mothers have gone back to school following or during their divorce. A year or two later they are always happier for the time they spent planning their future. The best way you can help your child have a positive work future is to provide her or him with a positive role model. Your divorce does not have to be a negative influence—you have choices. The message is *like what you do.*

# SPOUSE

Being a husband or wife is another adult role that is far in the future for your little one. Yet they are forming attitudes and opinions on marriage now that may affect their future relationships. It is normal and healthy to want to share your adult life with another person. To be able to take this step, you must be able to make an emotional commitment to that person. This commitment usually means you love your partner and are willing to share resources such as time, money, and interests with him or her. It also implies sexual and emotional fidelity.

You were married; your marriage was a commitment to share your adult life with your former spouse. You promised to do so "for better or worse, till death do you part." You now have experienced how a commitment made with affection and sincerity can change, shatter, and end. So have your children. You may be somewhat bitter and disillusioned and perhaps feel fearful about ever really trusting another adult. But watch your child. Little ones are usually very trusting; they give people a chance. You can learn from a child.

After a divorce it is very normal to feel hesitant and concerned about making another commitment to a new partner. For some, religious beliefs make remarriage impossible while their former spouse is alive unless they receive an official annulment of their former marriage. Yet it is quite natural to long for and desire to share your life with someone new. Before beginning a new relationship, however, please take the time you and your children need to heal from the hurts and disappointments your divorce produced. Try to resolve bitter feelings toward your former partner. Continuing bitterness and anger will contaminate any new relationship and will sap the positive energies needed to invest in a new partner. If you cannot bring yourself to put the past behind you for your own good, do it for your children's future ability to have successful marriages of their own.

The way you as a parent model your adult commitments will affect the type of commitments your child will make in the future. You were a partner to your child's other parent, and that commitment ended. You have other commitments, however, to your own parents, your child, your friends, your job. These commitments continue after the divorce. Has your child seen you keep your work, pay your bills, do special things for family and friends? Does your child see you respect and honor the divorce decree? If you meet another adult and make an emotional commitment to him or her, your child will draw ideas about commitments from observing that relationship.

These are tangible ways you can demonstrate to your children the ability to commit. As they reach adulthood, they will be able to use such positive experiences to help build their own adult relationships. Your divorce may result in your children's being somewhat cautious about marriage, but human beings usually want to have close committed relationships, so most children will grow up and marry. What you do will foster your children's ability to fulfill that commitment.


## PARENT

In addition to having a satisfying work role and a successful marriage, most adults want to be parents. Again, this is far in the future for your little one, but their parenting skills are being formed right now. To parent, an adult should be able to nurture a needy, dependent baby or child. Good parenting requires one to be able to remember how it was to be a child, yet stay in the adult role of setting appropriate and safe boundaries. Your example now will do more than anything else to help your own children be good parents when they grow up.

As you know, parenting has many rewards, but it is also a lot of hard work. The relationship with your child is a lifelong commitment that cannot be dissolved. Children truly are "nondivorceable." During the divorce process, the ability to parent is often strained. You may be experiencing considerable stress trying to adjust to the many changes and losses caused by your divorce and have little time and energy left to nurture your child. Unfortunately, just when parents are at this low ebb is when their children—also reacting to the losses and changes—need them most.

Recognizing your children's needs may help you be more available to them. Even when you are exhausted at the end of the day, for example, it's possible just to sit together to watch a short video, relax, or read a book after dinner and baths. If your children's grandparents or aunts and uncles live close by, perhaps they can supplement your parenting by having you all over to dinner or occasionally watching your children so that you can have some time to rest. Your local parish or congregation is also full of people willing to help out.

Joe, the father of 5-year-old Tommy, has become emotionally paralyzed by his divorce, which took place when Tommy was 18 months old. Joe cannot believe that he had lost his family. He fluctuates between rage and depression; his actions are often motivated by strategies to get back at Mia, his former wife. He occasionally skips visits with Tommy, hoping to make Mia suffer by having to stay home. He berates Mia in front to Tommy. Joe is trapped by his uncontrollable rage at being rejected; however, in the process he is not available to his son—an impressionable young person who very much needs to have an invested, caring father.

The deprivation of a positive role model may well strain Tommy's ability to nurture and parent when he is a father. His mother, grandparents, and kindergarten teacher are supplying emotional support. Tommy still may be a good father some day, but how much better for him if he could internalize a positive relationship with his own father.

The most important thing you can do to help your child grow up with the ability to parent is to put energy and effort into parenting your child now

## FRIEND AND CITIZEN

Family and work roles usually make up the emotional center of one's life. There are, however, many other roles that adults are required to fulfill—friend, consumer, neighbor, volunteer, and citizen. It is in these roles that we go beyond our own narrow interests and concerns and exhibit the spirit of service, sharing, and giving. Interaction with people outside of home and work help you feel connected to the community and the world. People who have an established network of friends and acquaintances through church or synagogue and community involvement usually adjust faster to divorce and other losses. Here again, it is up to you to provide the role model for your children.

Nancy had always attended church. Sunday worship was part of her weekly routine. After her divorce, she continued this pattern, and when the education department requested volunteer teachers she pondered whether she'd have the time and energy needed to prepare the weekly lessons. She works 30 hours a week and has two small children George, 2, and Sally, 3½. Her former husband takes the children to dinner every Wednesday and spends each Saturday with them. Perhaps, she thought, she could use Saturday afternoons to prepare. Nancy decided to give it a try.

Now every Sunday Nancy teaches a junior-high class. George and Sally are getting to know some of her students, and several of the young teens have offered to baby-sit for the children. Nancy did not volunteer to teach school because it would provide a positive role model for her children; she did it because she thought she wanted to give something back to the church. But George and Sally are receiving a positive message about adult behavior: giving to others is part of adult life.

Mark had been active in sports when he was in high school. He had been a good baseball player, but after he began working full-time he stopped playing. A few months after his divorce, Mark ran into an old high school friend, who asked whether Mark would be interested in being an assistant coach for the Little League in their town. Mark was missing his children, who had just moved 600 miles away. Impulsively Mark agreed, and the coaching turned out to be therapeutic for Mark and good for the team (they won their division). Mark sees his children, 6-year-old Marcia and 4-year-old Brad, every six weeks for long weekends and for the month of August. When he talks with them on the phone in between visits, he tells them about how his team is doing, and Marcia tells her Dad she is going to play T-ball next summer. Mark is illustrating to his children that he is the type of man who can give to children—his own and others.

Mark and Nancy are examples of how people use their connections and interests in the world outside of work and family to help them adjust to divorce. In both of these cases, the interests and friendships were established as a natural part of adult life. By their own example, Nancy and Mark were helping their children develop the skills necessary to form adult networks.

Encourage your children to be involved in activities and friendships. Allow birthday parties, swim lessons, church school. Support them in learning to help others. Take cookies to the nursing home, get a geranium for grandma, walk the dog next door. Such activities will help your child see the world as a place where one can gain support from others and in turn give support. Social interactions will help your children develop the skill to make and keep friends and be involved in their community when they are adults.

*A note of caution:* as your children become older, there will be many outside activities in which they can become involved, but it is important not to overenroll children. Some parents have their children in some activity every afternoon of the week and on sports teams on the weekends. This it too much structured activity. Children also need time to just *be*.

Your divorce does not need to hamper your children's ability to have satisfying friendships and community involvement. As with all preparation needed for adult roles, their parents' ability to emotionally recover from a divorce is one of the most critical factors in children's development. As you mend emotionally, you will be able to help your children engage in activities outside of the home.

# EXERCISE 10

*Imagining your child's future*

## FOR PARENTS

Write on a piece of paper these three columns: *How I Feel as a Worker (Spouse, Parent, Friend, and Citizen), What I'm Communicating to My Children,* and *What I Can Do.* Under each category, list how your current attitudes and actions are affecting your child's preparation for their adult roles. Are there any solutions you can initiate in the next week?

## RICH'S EXAMPLE

*Rich is a 45-year-old father with three children.*

| HOW I FEEL AS A WORKER | WHAT I'M COMMUNICATING | WHAT I CAN DO |
|---|---|---|
| 1. Bored | Being an accountant is a boring profession. | Ask my boss for a new assignment. |
| 2. Angry at not having the freedom to become a writer. | I don't have confidence in my own writing ability. | Send the short story I've been working on to a magazine. |

### AS A SPOUSE

| | | |
|---|---|---|
| 1. Gun-shy. I make jokes about marriage. | Marriage is a very risky and difficult business. | Talk to my parents and others who have a good marriage. Take the kids along. |
| | Being single is better. | Read some good books on marriage. |

### AS A PARENT

| | | |
|---|---|---|
| 1. Upset at only seeing the kids every other week. | Maybe I don't enjoy seeing them. | Get a better attitude during their visits. |
| | Their mother is to blame. | Ask my ex-wife to change the visitation agreement. |

| | | |
|---|---|---|
| 2. Really pleased to be a father. | My children feel loved. | Keep up the good work! |

## AS A FRIEND AND CITIZEN

| | | |
|---|---|---|
| 1. Sorry I've lost contact with my male friends. | You lose your friends when you get divorced. | Have a poker party with my friends while the kids are over. |
| | Friends aren't very important. | Talk to the kids about their friends. |
| 2. Disgusted with politicians. | All politicians are crooked. | Take the kids with me when I vote. |

## DISCUSSION

After Rich completed the exercise he realized he was beginning to develop some negative attitudes toward work, life, marriage, and even the government. After the divorce, it had seemed acceptable to mouth off about his feelings to work friends and family, but he knew he never liked being around negative, complaining, sarcastic people. Was he becoming one?

Rich's children were very important to him. He wanted his children to develop positive attitudes and good self esteem. Instead of complaining so much, Rich decided to monitor and modify his own reactions. He also decided to do something positive, so he joined a local health club. This may not seem like a big step, but it was. After three months of working out at the health club and actively working on his own responses to things, Rich felt happier. He has begun dating someone and is planning a fishing trip with friends.

## EXERCISE FOR INFANTS

Find a simple picture book. After your baby is fed and happy, sit him or her in your lap and read a story. An older infant may understand some of the words; a younger infant may just like being held, hearing you saying nice, calm words. The story should only be about three to five minutes long. If the baby still seems content, you might reread the story.

This exercise will begin to introduce books to your little one. Reading will be associated with the pleasure of you holding and talking to him or her.

## EXERCISE FOR TODDLERS

Go to the library or a bookstore and find a children's book that has pictures of grown-ups working. These books might have a farmer, police officer, grocer, teacher, and so on. Choose a simple book. This isn't for career counseling but just to begin to draw your child's attention to the outside world and jobs.

Read the book to your child. After you have completed the book ask her or him, "What do you want to do when you are a grown woman (or man)?" Be prepared for a fire fighter!

## EXERCISE FOR PRESCHOOLERS

Make a little book with your preschooler entitled "What People Do." Your book can be several pieces of typing paper folded in half. Think of grown-ups your child knows—Mommy, Daddy, Aunt Betty, Mr. Williams across the street, Miss Alice the preschool teacher. Then draw pictures of each of these people doing his or her job. If your child hesitates or doesn't feel confident, you can say, "I'll start it, and then you add the arms." Soon your child will most likely begin drawing the whole person. Your job is to print the name and job under the picture. You and your preschooler have just written a book!

# CONCLUSION

# THE ONGOING NATURE OF DIVORCE

*"Daddy, who is my family?"*

—4-year-old Jenny

The process of helping your child deal with your divorce will take a lifetime. Some people are still grappling with their parents' divorce well into mid-life. Children need to rethink and look at their parents' divorce over and over. At each age a child will have new questions and want to ask you about what happened. In the very early ages, children's main questions are about the family, and their fears are related to feeling secure and safe. Little children want to know where people are, when they will be home.

When children are 10 and 11, they often bring up the idea of living with the other parent. They are beginning to think about fairness and they look at how long I'm with Dad and how long I'm with Mom. Parents become very upset when this comes up and wonder what they have done wrong. Sometimes the answer is nothing; your child is in a developmental stage of understanding fairness.

Another critical period occurs when a child is between the ages of 15 to 17. At this age the adolescent is beginning to have experiences with love and sexuality. This may raise questions about the love and sexuality of his or her parents. "How did you meet Dad?" or "How could you sleep with another woman when you were still married to Mom?" are some examples of the things children may ask or want to know but are afraid to ask. It is important not to discount or avoid your children's questions; they are nearing adulthood and want honest, adult answers.

Your children may also need to reprocess the divorce when they are contemplating marriage or having their own children, when you remarry or move far away, or upon the occasion of a family tragedy—especially the death of one of the parents. All of these events are times of change and may trigger some unresolved emotions or questions related to the losses of the childhood family.

You, too, may be especially vulnerable in times of transition. Do not avoid these feelings or questions. Allow yourself and your children to continue the life-long healing, acceptance, understanding process.

## FINAL TIPS

Here are some final tips that may be useful to you and your children in successfully navigating the process that takes you from the pre-divorce family to your current family and into the future.

### 1. Take care of yourself—physically, emotionally, and spiritually.

Every aspect of your child's well-being depends on your being healthy. When the shock of divorce first descends, you may feel very tired. Get the rest you need. Eat well-balanced meals, and do not overconsume alcohol or coffee. If your tiredness persists, see your doctor.

For your emotional health, talk to others. It is crucial to share your anger, worry, frustration, sadness, and successes with an understanding friend. Also, try to begin helping someone else; see whether you, too, can listen. Finally, listen to your inner self—your spirit. God's grace is always there. If you find your church or synagogue a place where you sense peace and develop insights, continue to draw upon this support. The disillusionment of the divorce may have triggered a questioning of your religious beliefs. If you reject them, both you and your children will experience the additional loss of a spiritual base at a time when it is most needed.

All people need to sense a connection to their spirit, this connection may not have anything to do with formal religion. It has to do with an "inner knowing." There are many avenues to rebuild or to discover your spiritual dimensions: talking with an understanding member of the clergy, walking in the quiet woods, playing the piano, reading, meditating, writing, or taking care of an infant or elderly person are examples of how some people have found their spiritual selves. By listening to your inner self, you will discover a strength that can help you transcend this period of upheaval.

**2. Let go of intense anger toward your former spouse (your child's other parent) for the hurt that he or she caused.**

To help your child, the most important thing you can do—next to taking care of yourself—is to begin to dispel the anger toward your former spouse for all of the wrongs that you feel were perpetrated against you. It may be difficult, if not impossible, to take this step, but even the effort is helpful. This does not mean you should never have felt anger toward your former spouse. It is very healthy to feel and express anger when someone has hurt you. If the anger remains intense long after the hurtful incidents have occurred, however, it will definitely begin to interfere with your current mental well-being.

If you are not ready to give up your hate, then please try to set this as a future goal. If you remain filled with hate, your children will suffer more than anyone else.

**3. Try to build a co-parenting relationship with your former spouse.**

The children who fare the best after parental divorce are those whose parents can discuss and share matters that pertain to the children. This in no way implies that the divorced parents need to be best friends or chat about their personal lives. It means that both parents are entitled to know pertinent information about their children and participate in the important decisions affecting them.

Share concerns about your child's development. Tell each other about your child's fears and hopes. Do not wait for the other parent to build this type of communication—take the initiative yourself.

*A note of caution:* Do not use the concept of co-parenting to try to get closer to your former spouse for romantic or other personal interests. You would be using your child if you did. A co-parenting relationship should be just what the term implies—two parents who care very much about their child and share ideas and tasks to help in successfully raising the child.

**4. Provide and encourage alternative sources of support for your child.**

Children need and deserve all the love and affection that they can get. During the divorce process, there may be many times when your energy and time will be consumed by the many tasks and emotions you are facing. If your child has additional sources of love and affection, you can help him or her draw upon these during the times you are feeling drained.

Grandparents can be a wonderful source of support. If they are patient, grandparents will not mind taking your children on long outings and then stopping for ice cream. Let your parents—or your former spouse's parents—help nurture your child. Aunts, uncles, cousins, and friends are all additional possibilities for support for your children. Pets are also a source of love that children treasure. A family dog or cat does not talk back or take away toys and will often sit with children while they watch even the most inane TV cartoon.

**5. Encourage, but do not force, your child to express his or her feelings.**

Some children will not, or cannot, express their feelings. Some children simply cannot label their feelings—they know they feel something, but they don't know what to call it. Other children do not want to tell anyone their feelings; they want to protect their private emotions. Still other children have repressed their feelings about the divorce to such an extent that they really believe that they have no feelings about it.

Of course, everyone involved in a divorce has some feelings about it. If your child is unable or unwilling to express his or her feelings, do not push, pry, or intrude, but do continue to be open. Occasionally share what you think your child, or any child of a certain age, might be feeling in this situation. Allow your child the freedom not to comment.

Children sometimes can be open about their feelings with someone other than their parents. This other person might be a special friend, a sibling, a teacher, or a counselor. Do not take it as a personal slight if your child talks more easily to another about the divorce. It may be that he or she is trying to protect you or feels uncomfortable sharing positive feelings about the other parent. Be happy that your child can talk to someone. In time, your child may be able to share his or her feelings with you.

**6. Expect your child to have some feelings that are different from yours.**

If your child does share his or her feelings with you, remember that these feelings may not be similar to yours. Your child may think that your former spouse is very nice and express a desire to spend more time with him or her. If you have a bad look on your face when you hear these feelings expressed or try to talk your child out of feeling a certain way, he or she will eventually get the message that he or she can have feelings as long as they are exactly what you want them to be. When both parents send this message, children are put into a position in which they can never be honest. Try very hard not to convey this message to your child; permit your child to view the divorce from his or her own perspective.

**7. Do things with your child.**

During the process of divorce, you may often feel overwhelmed with things to do. It may seem like there is little time left to do fun activities with your child. It is important, however, to include time for your child. Perhaps on a Sunday afternoon you can stop for a treat or play a game after dinner. This type of attention will demonstrate to your children that despite the divorce they are going to continue to be cared for. It will help your children feel secure.

## 8. Do things with people other than your child.

Be careful not to let your child become the only person of interest in your life. You need adult friends, and you need to spend some time doing enjoyable adult activities without your child.

If you have other interests and friends, it will help your child's development. Your child will see you enjoying the outside world and will learn that it is possible to be a happy adult.

## 9. Encourage your child to develop and master his or her emerging abilities.

During your child's young years, he or she will begin to want to try out some new interests and develop new ideas and skills. If—because of parental divorce— the child does not have the energy, encouragement, or resources to invest in the development of these skills and interests, they may lie dormant and a valuable growth period will be missed.

Do not push your child into too many activities or overschedule your child's life. Rather, be in tune with your child and encourage him or her to build a base of experiences and skills that will lay the foundation for becoming a self-confident adult.

## 10. If either you or your child is having difficulties, consider seeking professional help.

Your divorce may be such a stressful process that as hard as you try to get your life functioning again you keep running into emotional, social, or financial problems. If you or your child continues to feel intense bitterness, sadness, or helplessness, perhaps a professional counselor would be helpful. Social workers and psychologists who work with divorcing families often know of resources available in your community. Just becoming linked with the right support (financial or legal assistance, child care, job placement, housing, health services, and so on) may lift a big weight off your shoulders.

Neither you nor your child has ever gone through what you are going through now. A professional counselor can help you and your child explore the disturbing aspects of divorce. Many people feel more comfortable discussing very private feelings and events with a stranger who is a professional. The relationship is confidential and a counselor will be listening and thinking only of your best interests.

Do not worry that you cannot afford professional help. Many counselors charge on a sliding scale (the fees are fixed on your ability to pay), and many religious agencies and mental-health facilities provide free counseling or will put you in contact with a counselor you can afford. If you don't know where to go, look in the phone book under *Family Counseling*, *Social Workers*, or *Psychologists*.

Another alternative is to join a support group. Various groups are organized by churches, synagogues, schools, and social service agencies. There are support groups for the recently divorced, those without partners for whatever reason, and single parents. Such groups allow you to share what you are going through with others who are experiencing or have been through similar situations. You might find you even want to continue in such a group to help others with their problems of divorce or single parenting.

Finally, use the exercises in this book whenever you think that they will be helpful to you or your child. You may find them useful again in two or three years, when your infant becomes a toddler or when your toddler becomes a preschooler and has additional questions or concerns about the divorce.

* * *

Being a parent is a lifelong commitment that will bring joy, anger, frustration, success, fun, worry, heartbreak, and satisfaction. The effort you have made to help your children accept and understand your divorce is just one of the many responsibilities of parenthood.

The fact that your are willing to make the special efforts involved in being a divorced parent is a large step toward fulfilling your commitment to your children.

# OTHER RESOURCES FROM ACTA PUBLICATIONS

*Kids Are Nondivorceable* by Sara Bonkowski. The version of this popular resource for divorced or separated parents with children ages 6-12. Deals with the special concerns and developmental stages of pre-adolescents. 126 pages, $7.95.

*Teens Are Nondivorceable* by Sara Bonkowski. The version of this popular resource for divorced or separated parents with children ages 12-18. Addresses specific issues faced by teenagers whose parents divorce. 160 pages, $7.95.

*Annulment: A Step-by Step Guide for Divorced Catholics* by Ronald T. Smith. This helpful, up-to-date guide provides practical information about each of the steps involved in the annulment process. 128 pages, $8.95.

*Divorce and Beyond* by James Greteman and Leon Haverkamp. This support-group program for newly divorced persons focuses on the "mourning period" of the divorce process and concentrates mainly on the divorced persons themselves, rather than on their role as parents. Participant's book, 132 pages, facilitator's manual, 80 pages, $5.95 each.

*Meditations (with Scripture) for Busy Moms* by Patricia Robertson. Insightful, down-to-earth reflections for each day of the year, paired with surprising and illuminating quotes from the Bible. 368 pages, $8.95.

*Meditations (with Scripture) for Busy Dads* by Patrick T. Reardon. A companion to the Moms book, just for Dads. 368 pages, $8.95.

**Available from booksellers or by calling 800-397-2282.**